CREATIVE READING FOR GIFTED LEARNERS:
a design for excellence

Michael Labuda, *Editor*
Jersey City State College

INTERNATIONAL READING ASSOCIATION
800 Barksdale Road   Newark, Delaware 19711

INTERNATIONAL READING ASSOCIATION

OFFICERS
1975-1976

President   Thomas C. Barrett, University of Wisconsin, Madison, Wisconsin

Vice-President   Walter H. MacGinitie, Teachers College, Columbia University, New York, New York

Vice-President Elect   William Eller, State University of New York, Buffalo, New York

Past President   Constance M. McCullough, Emeritus, San Francisco State University, San Francisco, California

Executive Director   Ralph C. Staiger, International Reading Association, Newark, Delaware

DIRECTORS

Term expiring Spring 1976
    Ira E. Aaron, University of Georgia, Athens, Georgia
    Lynette Saine Gaines, University of South Alabama, Mobile, Alabama
    Tracy F. Tyler, Jr., Robbinsdale Area Schools, Robbinsdale, Minnesota

Term expiring Spring 1977
    Roger Farr, Indiana University, Bloomington, Indiana
    Grayce A. Ransom, University of Southern California, Los Angeles, California
    Harry W. Sartain, University of Pittsburgh, Pittsburgh, Pennsylvania

Term expiring Spring 1978
    Roselmina Indrisano, Boston University, Boston, Massachusetts
    Ethna R. Reid, Exemplary Center for Reading Instruction, Salt Lake City, Utah
    Robert B. Ruddell, University of California, Berkeley, California

Copyright 1974 by the
International Reading Association, Inc.
Library of Congress Cataloging in Publication Data
Labuda, Michael.
    Creative reading for gifted learners.
    Includes bibliographies.
    1. Gifted children—Education—Reading—Addresses, essays, lectures. I. Title.
LC3993.5.L32   371.9'5   74-10850
ISBN 0-87207-717-9
Second printing, December 1975

CONTENTS

Foreword   iv

Introduction   v

PART I   CREATIVE PUPILS AND CREATIVE READING

- 2   Gifted and Creative Pupils: Reasons for Concern   *Michael Labuda*
- 8   Rationale for Fostering Creative Reading in the Gifted and the Creative   *Paul A. Witty*
- 25   Ingredients of A Creative Reading Program   *Walter B. Barbe*

PART II   SPECIAL CONSIDERATIONS

- 34   Parent Roles in Fostering Reading   *Edith H. Grotberg*
- 46   Language Programs for Young Children: Implications for the Creative and Gifted   *Dorothy S. Strickland*
- 51   Using Reading to Stimulate Creative Thinking in the Intermediate Grades   *Richard J. Smith*
- 60   Creativity in Secondary Schools   *Jo Brazell*

PART III   MATERIALS AND RESOURCES

- 70   Fostering Reading Growth for Gifted and Creative Readers at the Primary Level   *Carl J. Wallen*
- 80   Fostering Creative Reading at the Intermediate Level   *Robert E. Shafer*
- 97   Creativity Training Activities for Secondary School Students   *Joseph S. Renzulli* and *Carolyn M. Callahan*

PART IV   SUGGESTIONS FOR MEETING UNIQUE NEEDS

- 106   Make-Believe: An Important Affair   *Margaret S. Woods*
- 110   Creative Reading Can Be a Balance and an Anchor in Guiding the Gifted   *Ann F. Isaacs*
- 123   Fostering Creativity in Children Who Differ   *Michael Labuda* and *Helen J. James*

PART V   A LOOK AHEAD

- 138   Forging Ahead in Reading for Gifted and Creative Learners   *Michael Labuda*

FOREWORD

The responsibility of the school for meeting the particular needs of children whose ability places them at the lower end of the continuum is rarely challenged. Paradoxically, many teachers and administrators who support special provision for the retarded child cry "undemocratic" at the suggestion of a special program for his counterpart, the gifted child. Special funding for gifted programs is meagre or nonexistent in many areas.

The very title of this publication establishes the recognition by its authors of both the peculiar needs of the gifted student and his potential for superior achievement. The belief that giftedness presents unique educational needs and requires special programs, supported by rich and varied resources, is evidenced by the titles of the various chapters in the book.

The gifted pupil is a distinct challenge to both teachers and parents. The avidity with which this pupil seeks information and consumes instructional media may well burden the teacher beyond normal expectation. The need for an environment which will foster inquiry and stimulate the child to ever-widening interests may at times overwhelm even the most supportive parent. But the challenges of giftedness must not be ignored. The school and the home, each, must assume responsibility for providing experiences which will help every gifted child realize his or her potential.

The Association expresses its deep gratitude to the committee which in 1972 planned the Preconvention Institute from which *Creative Reading for Gifted Learners: A Design for Excellence* was developed. It is hoped that through this volume the educational programs and the lives of thousands of gifted children will be enriched.

Millard H. Black, *President*
International Reading Association
1973-1974

INTRODUCTION

It is the intent of this volume to indicate both the nature of children who possess traits of giftedness and creativity and the comprehensive educational procedures required to meet their needs.

Part One attends to two elements: the characteristics of gifted and creative children and an explication of the meaning of a creative reading program. Labuda gives an overview of the reasons for concerns about gifted and creative learners. The summary of research by Witty highlights the needs of gifted children and the meaning of creative reading. Barbe explains the scope of a creative reading program, including the goals, resources and materials, and skills to be learned.

Part Two covers important aspects of creativity and creative reading to be considered as teachers implement their instructional programs. Grotberg presents views of home and parent influences on gifted children and describes ways in which parents and teachers may work together to provide for these children. Strickland delineates the elements of a total language arts program for young children (K-3), substantiating the need for oral language development as a foundation for reading skills development. Smith discusses reading as a thinking process and then outlines the special characteristics and reading needs of intermediate grade children, concluding with suggested procedures for meeting needs that may be relevant to educational programs at all levels. The problems of secondary pupils are reviewed by Brazell, followed by some of the solutions which teachers may utilize for gifted and creative students. Teachers of the middle school grades (6-9) will find a wealth of suggestions for individualization of their classroom programs in the articles by Smith and Brazell.

Part Three proposes specific materials and resources that have fostered reading growth for pupils in grades K-12. Wallen describes reading goals, materials, and skills for primary grade children; the review of current approaches will enable teachers to select ideas suitable for their own programs. Shafer explains ways to give intermediate grade pupils a broad program involving the total language arts; teachers of grades 5-8 will find many ideas for improvement of pupils' total communication skills. Renzulli and Callahan postulate four principles underlying creativity training of secondary pupils; they then explain training activities that will enable older youths to produce creatively.

Part Four gives attention to the unique needs of certain gifted and creative children. Woods urges teachers to capitalize on children's natural tendency to "make-believe" and demonstrates ways to enhance the growth of children's imaginative solutions to problems. Isaacs details the needs of gifted children as they cope with their own uniqueness in what is largely a conforming environment; after reviewing a variety of general approaches that provide guidance to such children in and through reading activities, she concludes the chapter with an extensive list of enriching activities. Labuda and James examine the needs of minority group children and learning disabled children who give evidence of giftedness or creativity; they cite the needs of these children and propose implications for their education, concluding with examples of creative production by children who differ in multiple ways.

In Part Five, Labuda appropriately concludes the volume with a glimpse of encouraging trends and offers suggestions for needs in the future.

Helen J. James
The University of West Florida

PART ONE

CREATIVE PUPILS AND CREATIVE READING

This section provides the reader with the basic *rationale* for a concern about improving reading instruction for gifted and creative learners. The focus is on two elements: defining the gifted and creative learner and defining creative reading.

The topics have been sequenced to furnish a sound foundation for curriculum adaptation. First, there is a general overview of the basic problem; evidence cited from research supports the premise that there are gifted and creative pupils of diverse nature and that creative reading can play an important role in providing for the needs of these pupils. The considerable documentation provided in these chapters attempts to demonstrate the value of a creative reading program for the gifted or at least to provide the arguments for the provision of special reading instruction for a number of talented learners in each classroom.

M.L.

GIFTED AND CREATIVE PUPILS: REASONS FOR CONCERN

Michael Labuda
Jersey City State College

Interest in special educational programs for the gifted and creative is not new. Greatness in human existence, aspiration, and achievement is a theme which has been treated since prehistoric times in literature and art and more recently through scholarly analysis and research. Throughout history, recognition and encouragement have definitely depended upon the nature of the gift and the cherished beliefs existing at that time. However, at all times, including the present, provisions have been unsystematic and inadequate.

The earliest definition of gifted children was based on objective criteria and was stated in terms of IQ derived from an intelligence test. Later, to justify creative behavior, the definition most commonly accepted was one in which consistently remarkable performance was achieved in any potentially valuable area. More recently the advisory panel to the U.S. Commissioner of Education established the following definition for the purpose of Federal education programs (*1*).

> Gifted and talented children are those by virtue of outstanding abilities capable of high performance. These are children who require differentiated educational programs and/or services beyond those normally provided by the regular school program in order to realize their contribution to self and society.
>
> Children capable of high performance include those with demonstrated achievement and/or potential ability in any of the following areas, singly or in combination:
>
> 1. general intellectual ability
> 2. specific academic aptitude
> 3. creative or productive thinking
> 4. leadership ability
> 5. visual and performing arts
> 6. psychomotor ability
>
> It can be assumed that utilization of these criteria for identification of the gifted and talented will encompass a minimum of 3 to 5 percent of the school population.

> Evidence of gifted and talented abilities may be determined by a multiplicity of ways. These procedures should include objective measures and professional evaluation measures which are essential components of identification.
>
> Professionally qualified persons include such individuals as teachers, administrators, school psychologists, counselors, curriculum specialists, artists, musicians, and others with special training who are also qualified to appraise pupils' special competencies.

The advisory panel cautions the use of an operational definition which is too specific and does not allow for flexibility. In their report to the U.S. Commissioner of Education, they offer the following as an operational definition (1).

> Generally, the following evidence would indicate special intellectual gifts or talent:
>
>> Consistently very superior scores on many appropriate standardized tests.
>>
>> Judgment of teachers, pupil personnel specialists, administrators, and supervisors familiar with the abilities and potentials of the individual.
>>
>> Demonstration of advanced skills, imaginative insight, and intense interest and involvement.
>>
>> Judgment of specialized teachers (including art and music), pupil personnel specialists, and experts in the arts who are qualified to evaluate the pupil's demonstrated and/or potential talent.

Gifted and creative children at all levels are being denied the intellectual stimulation everyone deserves in a democratic society. These children will not triumph over mediocre education programs and achieve at a superior level without special assistance. According to the democratic tradition, man is the measure of all things and the all-powerful force in society. Mead (3) has called it a "fix-it" society in which whatever inferiorities man has demonstrated can be easily fixed. There appears to be a colossal amount of faith that average or below average children can approximate common man, while the gifted and creative—since they are functioning above the potentiality of this common man theme—are allowed to drift. This misfortune has resulted in an incalculable loss to society of leadership potential.

Gifted and creative children do exist outside our affluent society. In fact, among the greatest potential sources waiting to be tapped are those children whose gifts are disguised by clothing, dialect, or cultural differences. From early childhood, gifted children give indications of superior intellectual ability. Typically, half of the gifted have taught themselves to read, with some children reading as early as age two. These children may walk and talk at an earlier age than other children and in other ways indicate that they are more advanced for their age. Since they are more alert and learn more quickly, they are advanced in visual, auditory, language, and listening behavior skills. Parents can share with the school an important responsibility in helping their children to achieve their maximum potential. They can read to their children; encourage originality, ask questions, and provide a variety of experiences; stimulate creative thinking and problem solving; be a real companion; and demonstrate a love for reading by reading themselves. Once aware of their role, all parents, regardless of their socioeconomic levels, may stimulate the learning of their children.

The majority of researchers favor a continuous screening and search program. At the minimum, there must be an annual reevaluation so that educational planning and placement will fulfill the educational needs of all gifted and creative children. Furthermore, in this search, there must be multiple measures of identification, including intelligence, achievement, talent, and creativity.

While the demonstrated and documented characteristics of the gifted and creative provide adequate information for planning educational experiences, little effort has been made to identify gifted and creative children at the preschool and elementary levels. In many instances, giftedness can be discerned in the preschool years. As children display signs of readiness for reading, teachers must be willing to accept their cues and begin to teach reading on the level at which the child may profit from the various procedures. In school systems where efforts have been made for them to satisfy their desires for knowledge and performance, there is a definite relationship between educational opportunities and adjustment. All too often, however, the programs consist of one or two special classes, taken along with standard requirements. Problems such as mass transportation, pollution, and the energy crisis will yield only to the most sophisticated and well trained minds.

A comparison of gifted and creative children with their age peers reveals that they have a longer attention span, a persistent curiosity, a desire to learn rapidly, a good memory, an awareness and appreciation of people and things, a wide range of interests, and the ability to solve the many problems besetting society. They value independence which is task and contribution oriented, reject conformity, hold high social ideals and values, and possess individuality and originality. Some in this group will need help in moving from primary reading habits to low maturity reading levels. Others are ready to read in a mature way with good speed and for a number of different purposes.

Exceptional capacities create problems for most people and for young children in particular. Since their ideas are advanced, these children sometimes do not fit into situations with others of their own age and find themselves marginal and isolated. However, since it is human to enjoy social association, the gifted and creative tend to relate to older companions and to games which involve individual skills or intellectual pursuits. This unique population has demonstrated the need for special programs to foster their unique abilities. Rather than less guidance, they need more guidance when compared to their peers. In good special programs, they have shown remarkable improvement in involvement and interest in learning. Many perform superbly in community groups, student government, and athletics. Their diverse pursuits require a balanced reading program which encompasses reading for many different purposes in many types of materials; e. g., they read for pleasure, for study in content areas, for classroom activities, for sharing ideas, and as a basis for creative activities. In the past, good programs on the secondary level have surpassed those being offered on the elementary levels.

Within recent years researchers have given increased attention to the topic of creativity. Many tests have been developed to measure creativity; presently there is considerable knowledge of the nature of the creative person and creativity tests beyond the exploratory stages are available. It is depressing and almost inconceivable that 57.5 percent of all schools surveyed in a recent U.S. Office of Education survey reported having no gifted pupils (*1*). Whether the responses were the result of ignorance or apathy, it seems clear that there are too few opportunities for the gifted and creative to develop to their fullest potential.

During the 1970s, we have seen education embark on an era of appropriate education for a diverse people in a diverse world. It is impossible to claim to be interested in the individual child and then do nothing about his uniqueness. Education can be appropriate only when it fulfills the needs of each individual. Those responsible for the educational system as it exists in many communities today must be pushed beyond their present efforts. Approximately 80,000 gifted and creative children are receiving education which is appropriate for their unique abilities (*2*). In a total school population of over 52 million elementary-secondary population, service for 80,000 gifted and creative falls vastly short, by any conservative estimate, of appropriate education for all. In some instances, less rigidity and formality have fostered more alertness to individual differences. In most instances, this more imaginative structure has fallen short of the requirements for the gifted and creative. Rearranging furniture and knocking down walls is not enough; provision should be made for open access to advanced materials and development of independence, originality, and creative expression.

Today, teachers are provided with numerous new and exciting instructional materials that encourage growth. However, to be utilized fully by all pupils, materials must be at an appropriate level of difficulty for each individual. The determination of a program should be based upon the needs of particular children in each individual situation. Students will be led to the fullest development of their abilities only if teachers use materials in relation to the needs of each individual. Even with traditional materials, gifted and creative pupils can be challenged to grow when assignments are based on achievement levels.

The reading needs of the gifted and creative differ in many respects from those of other groups; indeed, needs are different for each child within each group. The gifted child can develop to his maximum if he is taught to think and act in a creative manner. Strict regimentation does not create an atmosphere conducive to creative thinking and creative reading. The child must be encouraged to express himself freely and not feel restrained because of nonconformity or divergent thinking. This can best be accomplished in a classroom atmosphere of freedom—freedom which permits the child to accomplish his learning task at his own level and his own rate. Perhaps teachers need to think in terms of encouraging tomorrow's minds rather than yesterday's minds, a gamut that gives children freer range to focus on the unsolved part of the curriculum, rather than only on the solved parts. There is a need to implant enough knowledge to cause children to think and then to encourage them to expand their understanding through unaccustomed avenues of intellectual activity. Since the gifted may become zealous readers with many special interests, free access to many supplementary materials should be provided. Interests will expand through exposure to interesting ideas, activities, and materials. A number of processes, abilities, and purposes will be employed and undoubtedly will soon embrace many different skills, concepts, and attitudes.

SUMMARY

A reorientation of public attitude concerning education of the gifted and creative child from all socioeconomic levels must take on a new impetus. Myths must be demolished regarding the ideas that gifted children need less guidance, will triumph over mediocre programs, and come only from affluent society. The extension of opportunities to the gifted is not undemocratic; in a democratic society we must provide opportunities for all gifted and creative children so that they may be permitted to grow to their fullest capacity.

In general, the research and literature on reading instruction support the idea that gifted and creative pupils can attain the highest level of ability—that of evaluative and creative behavior—if they gain the skills that make them independent. From early age to adulthood, maximum growth in reading and study skills is not only desirable but essential for them.

The needs of gifted and creative students are evident; they deserve the best and most fulfilling educational experiences we can offer. They deserve programs characterized by balance and breadth and which offer an opportunity for specialization in line with children's interests at all levels. By extending and enriching opportunities in reading, educators can take a significant step forward in providing the kind of education the gifted so justly deserve; the kind of education that will enhance their growth and the fulfillment of their potential.

References
1. *Education of the Gifted and Talented.* Report to Congress by the U.S. Commissioner of Education and background papers submitted to the U.S. Office of Education. Washington, D.C.: U.S. Government Printing Office, 1972. (72-502 0)
2. Marland, Sidney P., Jr. "Our Gifted and Talented Children: A Priceless National Resource," *Intellect*, October 1972.
3. Mead, Margaret. "The Gifted Child in American Culture Today," *Journal of Teacher Education*, 5 (September 1954).

RATIONALE FOR FOSTERING CREATIVE READING IN THE GIFTED AND THE CREATIVE*

Paul A. Witty, Emeritus
Northwestern University

IDENTIFICATION OF GIFTED AND CREATIVE PUPILS

After the widespread use of intelligence tests, attention in our schools centered on the range of abilities within every classroom and the need for adaptations and extensions of the curriculum to care for the individual differences. Special provisions were made for slow learning and retarded pupils, and efforts were occasionally undertaken to enrich the experiences of the gifted (*3, 24*).

Initial Research Efforts

The gifted child was generally considered to be one of high IQ, a conviction that long continued in education. Comprehensive studies of Lewis M. Terman, following the pioneer work of Alfred Binet, led to the testing of large numbers of children and youth and to assignment of children to various categories of ability. Children earning IQs of 130 and higher, designated as gifted, constituted about one percent of elementary school pupils in the early surveys, while somewhat higher percentages were later reported. Pupils with IQs of 140 and higher were assigned to the category "genius" or "near genius."

Large scale genetic investigations of the gifted were made about 1920. Reports of these studies were published in several volumes and were summarized by Terman and Oden. Terman (*15*) stated that the following findings were most significant:

> ...children of IQ 140 or higher are, in general, appreciably superior to unselected children in physique, health, and social adjustments; markedly superior in moral attitudes as measured either by character tests or by trait ratings; and vastly superior in their mastery of school subjects as shown by a three-hour battery of achievement tests. In fact, the typical child of the group had mastered the school subjects to a point

---

*This manuscript is based on and extended from the IRA publication *Reading for the Gifted and the Creative Student*, Paul Witty, Editor (1971), and "Fostering Creative Reading" by Paul Witty in *Highlights for Teachers*, Number 25.

about two grades beyond the one in which he was enrolled, some of them three or four grades beyond.

Follow-up investigations were made over a period of 30 years. These studies showed that the academic superiority of the gifted pupil was maintained and that "the promise of youth" was realized to a conspicuous degree insofar as superiority in school was concerned. Thus, Terman stated:

> ...close to 90 percent entered college and 70 percent graduated. Of those graduating, 30 percent were awarded honors and about two-thirds remained for graduate work.

Further investigations of the gifted as young adults, compared with studies of proven geniuses, convinced Terman that:

> ...the genius who achieves the highest eminence is one whom intelligence tests would have identified as gifted in childhood.

Although the results of the present writer's studies of gifted children agreed closely with those of Terman, he differed sharply in the interpretation of the data. He questioned whether one is justified in assuming that a high IQ may be used to predict creative behavior or the achievements of the genius. Moreover, he emphasized the importance of factors such as interest, drive, opportunity, and early education in affecting the nature and extent of individual attainment.

Clearly, these studies of gifted pupils demonstrated the value of the IQ in selecting one type of child for whom promise of academic attainment is great and for whom appropriate opportunities are needed. It became clear that enrichment of various kinds was beneficial in both the elementary and the secondary school. However, the amount of such provisions has been, and continues to be, meager.

Recognition of the Importance of Early Learning

Terman and his associates emphasized the importance of hereditary factors in producing relatively stable IQs. Although these investigators mentioned the significance of opportunities for early learning, their studies of the gifted dealt largely with pupils of school age after early childhood had passed. Recently, the importance of the early years has been brought vividly to our attention. Thus, Pines (*11*) has stated:

> Millions of children are being irreparably damaged by our failure to stimulate them intellectually during their crucial years—from birth to six. Millions of others are being held back from their true potential.

Undeniably, there has been neglect of intellectual stimulation for young children, not only in the home but in the nursery school or preschool center (*28*). It is being asserted that the provision of rich and varied experiences in early childhood will increase learning ability and heighten intelligence. It is believed that a more general provision of such opportunities would raise the incidence of superior children residing in areas in which deprivation and disadvantage prevail.

Findings Concerning Children Who Read Early

Investigators have recently stressed the potentiality of children for learning to read at early ages. The possibility was long ago recognized by scholars who suggested that perhaps age four was the time most desirable for beginning reading instruction. It was proposed that reading instruction be started earlier, but opposition was great since most educators appeared to believe that readiness for reading necessitated the attainment of a mental age of six years or more. In 1966, Durkin's study (*5*) of children who read early caused many thoughtful people to reexamine this issue. Durkin reported that children in a group, one-third of whom had IQs below 110, entered the first grade with superior achievement in reading and maintained their lead over a five-year period. Notable was Durkin's description of the parents of the early readers. They were characterized as having respect for learning and supporting its encouragement in very young children.

In the writer's studies (*25, 26, 27*) at Northwestern University, the parents of gifted children who read early appeared to be similarly concerned about the achievement of their children during the early crucial years. These parents frequently read aloud to their children, fostered language expression, provided varied books and materials, and showed by their own behavior a respect for reading. Some of these parents encouraged their children to write, spell, and record their experiences in simple forms. Under these conditions, more than half of the gifted group learned to read, without undue pressure, before starting school.

Identification of the Creative Pupil

It has been found that the use of standard measures of intelligence will not enable one to identify the creative pupil with success. Recognition of this fact is not new (*22*). Indeed, many years ago, the present writer found that the correlation was low between IQ and performance judged to be highly creative. It was also observed that most of the materials generally utilized in the intelligence test were not suitable to elicit novel, imaginative, or creative responses. Undoubtedly, the intelligence test has helped in the identification of one kind of ability, but it does not enable one to identify creative pupils accurately.

Several other investigators have found that if one were to limit his selection to pupils of very high IQ, he would fail to include many of the most creative pupils (*6, 18*). Accordingly, efforts have been made to develop tests of creativity (*6, 17*). The work of Guilford (*8*) has stimulated a prolonged search for the components of creativity with attention to factors such as sensitivity to problems, fluency, flexibility, and originality. Research workers have devised tests to measure some of these components and have compared creative and high IQ pupils. Critics have stressed certain limitations in the tests of creativity and have cited the need for caution in using them. They point out that, although the correlation between the tests of creativity and IQ is low, as in the Getzels-Jackson studies (*6*), the correlation is also low between the various subtests in the creativity assembly. Hence, the designation of two groups of subjects, one the "intelligent" and the other the "creative," is questioned. Such criticism undoubtedly will lead to the extension of the studies and clarification of important issues (*14*).

Particularly needed is further study of various kinds of creativity, their measurement, and their relationships. Indeed, as Guilford states:

> It would be risky to conclude that because a child shows signs of creativity in art he should also be creative in mathematics or in science, or vice versa.

Search for a Variety of Creative Abilities

Despite the limitations of tests of creativity, one may recognize a number of practical approaches to employ in the identification of children whose promise of creativity is great. For example, in a study made by the writer (*23*), the remarkable film, ***The Hunter and The Forest***, was shown in many schools throughout the United States. The film has no commentary but utilizes a musical score and the sounds of animals and birds as accompaniments.

After the pupils had seen the film, they were asked to write a commentary, story, or poem about it. Approximately 10 percent of the pupils wrote so effectively that their products suggested unique creative ability as judged by three experts who examined the work to select compositions of creative superiority and qualitative excellence. The agreement of these judges was close in regard to the top creative pupils. Moreover, in several analyses, it was shown that if only a high IQ had been used to identify the gifted, a large number of the top creative pupils would have been excluded. It was also found that many of the outstanding compositions were written by pupils who had not previously been observed as having unusual aptitude in writing. If additional outstanding performance corroborated this first demonstration of exceptional ability, these pupils would be considered potentially gifted in this area (*22, 23*).

Because of such findings, the present writer proposed that a potentially gifted child be considered as any child whose performance in a worthwhile type of human endeavor is repeatedly or consistently remarkable. He suggested that a search be made, not only for pupils of high verbal ability, but also for those of unusual promise in mathematics and sciences, writing, art, music, drama, mechanical ability, and social leadership.

Scholars are increasingly recognizing the prevalence of undiscovered talent and are initiating a quest for multiple talents in children and youth. For example, Taylor (*14*) has described a multiple talent search by the Utah Task Force. And Torrance (*17, 18*) has employed effectively a number of approaches to find creative pupils.

Social Adjustments of Gifted and Creative Pupils

We have already noted the characteristics of some gifted children who have been identified by intelligence tests. In addition to their superiority in school work, the high IQ children were found typically to be well-adjusted socially and to get along well with their peers. Creative pupils were found typically to be less well-adjusted and to have difficulties in peer relationships. Thus, Torrance (*17*) states:

> Many of the highly creative individuals are disturbing elements in classroom groups in elementary schools. The problem of teachers and guidance workers resolves itself into one of helping highly creative individuals maintain those characteristics which seem essential to the development of creative talent and, at the same time, helping them acquire skills for avoiding, or reducing to a tolerable level, the peer sanctions.

The findings of Torrance are supported in a study by Victor and Mildred G. Goertzel (*7*). These authors chose 400 persons, acknowledged as eminent by a high frequency of biographies currently written about them. Concerning their childhood, the authors state:

> They showed their greatest superiority in reading ability; many read at the age of four. Almost all were early readers of good books. They were original thinkers and had scant patience with drill and routine. They were likely to be rejected by their playmates and had parents who valued learning.

The authors indicate also that "Three out of five of the four hundred had serious school problems" and conclude:

> Now as in the days of the Four Hundred, the child who is both intelligent and creative remains society's most valuable resource. When we learn to work with him instead of against him, his talents may reward us in ways beyond our ability to imagine.

Recommendations for Reading Instruction of the Gifted

The evidence of research makes clear some of the characteristics of gifted and creative pupils. In terms of these characteristics the following practices in reading instruction and guidance appear to be worthy of implementation.

1. The guidance of the reading of the gifted child should begin at home. It has been found that gifted children who are able to read on entering school have parents who often read aloud to them and patiently answer children's questions about words. Their homes sometimes contain children's magazines, picture and storybooks, dictionaries, and encyclopedias. The parents themselves turn to reading for information and pleasure (*21*). Some are particularly interested in providing a stimulating environment and in encouraging learning during the crucial early years.

2. Some gifted pupils are able to read on entering kindergarten and they should be given opportunities to apply and develop their reading abilities. Unfortunately, reading has been tabooed in some kindergartens. This practice should be abandoned and the importance of reading and reading readiness should be acknowledged as a vital aspect of the curriculum. Since many gifted children will not be able to read on entering school, they should be offered a broad background of first-hand experience coupled with varied forms of language expression. They should be encouraged to decode, pronounce, write, and spell words which appear in their own experience charts. If a gifted child is able to read on entering the first grade, he should be encouraged to do so from varied sources that are individually suitable and appealing. He should not be limited to typical, routine basal instruction and unnecessary readiness activities. Emphasis should be placed on reading as a thinking and communicating process (*23*).

3. Varied approaches may be used in the initial reading instruction of the gifted. An effective way to introduce children to reading as a thinking process is to have them tell a story depicted by pictures of a familiar incident arranged in sequence. The pupils may then be encouraged to tell stories from picture books devoid of text (i.e., books in the **Little Owl Series** published by Holt, Rinehart and Winston). Reading may be appreciated further as a way of communicating in activities such as the "reading" of faces, signs, and illustrations (*18*). Each child's own words may then be recorded in his own story and used as his first reading material. Teachers who follow the language experience approach encourage children to make their own books as initial reading material. Experience charts are widely employed by others. Individualized reading instruction may also foster the use of self-selection and pacing in reading. Varied books on

topics of interest will be read by the gifted child who will find satisfaction in sharing his discoveries in reading with his classmates. Under these conditions, the gifted child's ability and interest develop rapidly. By the time he reaches the fourth grade, he usually will have become an avid reader (*25*).

4. A special problem is presented to the teacher who seeks to enrich the reading experience of the gifted child within the regular classroom. The writer of this chapter (*21*) has described successful efforts of teachers to deal with the problem created by the wide range of ability within the typical classroom. In such classrooms, interest inventories may be administered and the results used to set up small flexible groups to explore each area or topic of interest. Reading materials related to each topic may be made available on varied levels of difficulty. Gifted pupils may make their contributions from reading the more advanced subject matter on each topic. This strategy is being used effectively in subject areas such as science or social studies.

5. The importance of interests should be fully recognized. Studies have shown that most gifted children have rich and varied interests in which reading can readily be related; however, there are some gifted pupils in whom wholesome interests are few. In these cases, efforts should be made to create new patterns of interest through direct experience, the use of films and filmstrips, and other activities. Some gifted children tend to concentrate their reading in a single specialized area such as science. Others make little use of varied types of reading materials. Teachers and librarians should work together to assist such pupils in the development of balanced programs of reading. Here again, the interest inventory may be employed to advantage (*24, 25*).

6. There is clearly a need for reading experience that will help gifted and creative students meet their personal and social problems with success. In this effort, the reading of narratives and biographies has proved helpful. Although such pupils may not always be helped by reading alone, reading has proved beneficial, particularly when it is accompanied by discussion and relevant experiences (*25*).

7. Gifted children should be encouraged to enjoy poetry, an area sometimes neglected by them. Anthologies of poetry such as *Favorite Poems—Old and New* (Doubleday), collected by Helen Ferris, and Untermeyer's *Story Poems* (Washington Square Press) are being employed effectively. Children should be given opportunities not only to enjoy poetry, but also to write poetry. In many innovative programs for the gifted, creative writing is featured as a correlate to reading; strategies such as the use of unfinished stories, the writing of

Haiku and *Tanka*, and other techniques are employed to motivate creative expression (*23, 28*).

MEETING THE NEEDS OF GIFTED AND CREATIVE PUPILS: THE ROLE OF CREATIVE READING

Some scholars believe that a great stimulus in the education of the gifted would result from the general inauguration of a program of creative reading (*4, 18*). One may think of reading in two ways: The first stresses pronunciation and simple comprehension through the accurate identification of words and thought units. Creative reading, the second way, may be regarded as the highest and most neglected aspect of reading (*12, 18*).

In the first practice, exercises requiring study of the meanings of words and phrases in accord with context are helpful in establishing accurate perception. Thus, appreciation of the literal meaning of passages is enhanced. Emphasis on skills such as getting the central thought of a paragraph or noting details is relevant in this endeavor. This practice also involves the pupil's sensing the relationships of the material or ideas perceived to his background of experience. These assimilative responses will include widely varied reactions because of the greatly differing backgrounds of pupils. The reactions are, to a considerable degree, "convergent" in nature. Only to a small degree do they extend beyond the facts presented, and constitute "divergent production" (*18*).

We may consider creative reading to be a thinking process in which new ideas are originated, evaluated, and applied. Divergent and varied responses, not right answers, are goals as thinking transpires and conclusions are reached. Finally, the pupil evaluates his conclusions and seeks to extend and use them (*9, 12, 18*).

Explanation of Creative Reading as a Process

Some advocates of creative reading, influenced by Guilford's writing (*8*) on the *Structure of Intellect*, stress mental operations such as cognition, memory, convergent production, divergent production, and evaluation.

Torrance (*18*) defines the foregoing operations as follows:

> The first, *cognition*, includes discovery, awareness, recognition, comprehension, or understanding. The second, *memory*, refers to retention or storage, with some degree of availability, of information. Then there are two types of *productive thinking* in which something is produced from what has been cognized or memorized: *Divergent production* or the generation of information from given information, where emphasis is upon variety and quantity of output from the same source, and *convergent production* or the generation of information where emphasis is

upon achieving unique or conventionally accepted best outcomes (the given information fully determines the response). The fifth operation is ***evaluation***, reaching decisions or making judgments concerning the correctness, suitability, adequacy, desirability, and so forth of information in terms of criteria of identity, consistency, and goal satisfaction.

Students in the area of creative reading frequently emphasize the significance of convergent and divergent production. Convergent production, as we have indicated, involves the use of reading largely to obtain correct meanings while divergent production involves individual response that implies several possible answers wherein no single response is correct and wherein novel, original, and imaginative reactions are anticipated (*29*).

In his book, **Gifted Children in the Classroom**, Torrance states:

> When a person reads creatively, he is sensitive to problems and possibilities in whatever he reads. He makes himself aware of the gaps in knowledge, the unsolved problems, the missing elements, things that are incomplete or out of focus. To resolve this tension, so important in the creative thinking process, the creative reader sees new relationships, creates new combinations, synthesizes relatively unrelated elements into a coherent whole, redefines or transforms certain pieces of information to discover new uses, and builds onto what is known.

Another approach to reading also stresses creative reading as a thinking process, but the approach is somewhat different from the Guilford emphasis. Russell (*12*) suggests that

> ...children, adolescents, and adults typically read at four overlapping levels. In ascending order these are
> 1. word identification
> 2. casual skimming
> 3. reading for exact, literal meanings
> 4. creative reading for
>   a. implied and inferred meanings
>   b. appreciative reactions
>   c. critical evaluations

The first three types of reading are primarily efforts to assimilate the facts presented and their literal meaning. In word identification, the reader is concerned primarily about pronouncing each word successfully. The act involves not only phonetic and structural analysis but may also require the use of context clues in reading a passage accurately. The second level, skimming, is an attempt to obtain general ideas or impressions or to find certain facts in a presentation, or even to decide whether a passage should be read more carefully. This type of reading is often stressed in speed reading courses. Exact or literal meanings are sought in the next more demanding level. Textbook assignments frequently require this type of literal reading. All three levels emphasize convergent reactions in which "right" answers are sought.

Creative reading, on the other hand, requires active response which extends beyond the literal meaning or the answers found in textbooks. The first three levels of reading are involved, but the emphasis is on higher level responses and thinking (*12*). Creative reading resembles creative thinking in that it helps the reader gain new insights by enabling him to evaluate an hypothesis and reach a conclusion. Thus, the creative reader employs reading in various types of thinking. He goes beyond the facts and considers their meanings, implications, and usefulness (*12, 18*).

In the levels referred to we may recognize a development from reaction of the **convergent** (or correct answer) type to response of the higher **divergent** form as shown in the following progression which is set forth by Russell (*12*):

> Accurate perception of words and thought units
> Understanding literal meanings
> Integration of ideas with past experience
> Seeing implied relationships, hidden meanings, reacting to symbols
> Developing new ideas either appreciative or critical
> Using these new ideas in other activities

Another approach to the encouragement of teaching reading as a thinking process is based on Bloom's ***Taxonomy of Educational Objectives*** (*2*) in which objectives are classified in six categories. The classification is arranged according to the complexity of the operations as follows: knowledge, comprehension, application, analysis, synthesis, and evaluation (*9*). Jarolimek (*10*) uses this sequence in suggestions for teaching social studies skills:

> One large group of such skills deals basically with a variety of intellectual operations. Thinking, asking questions, using language, solving problems, interpreting stories and pictures, and making simple analyses are a few examples of skills of this type. In most cases, they are related to the informational content of the program. They do not deal basically with **getting** information but with interpreting, processing, and using information.

For teaching such social studies skills, Jarolimek recommends the use of questions which call for divergent responses, not correct answers.

In fostering creative reading generally, as in the cultivation of social studies skills, the use of questions plays an important role. In fact, Smith (*13*) points out that creative reading "could be taught best through the skillful use of questions." Moreover, he defines creativity "according to Bloom's (1956) delineation of the cognitive level of synthesis. Applied to reading, this means that ideas acquired from a reading selection are combined with ideas acquired elsewhere in a purposeful search for a new product, pattern, or structure."

Smith suggests that the expression of noncreative and creative responses may be prompted by "convergent questions" and by "divergent questions." He presents two lists labeled "Convergent Questions" and "Divergent Questions." If the teacher follows the first list, he would tend to elicit noncreative responses (convergent) while use of the second list would encourage creative responses (divergent). The somewhat modified lists follow:

Convergent Questions	Divergent Questions
1. Ask only for information that is in the story.	1. Ask for information not in the story.
2. Do not ask for the reader's personal ideas.	2. Ask for the reader's personal ideas.
3. Ask for a correct answer that can be determined by analyzing the story.	3. Evoke open-ended, inferred responses.
4. Focus on the author's meaning.	4. Focus on what the reader can add.

The Role of the Teacher

The extent to which children develop creative abilities in reading depends largely upon their teacher. From the first, good teachers encourage children to question the facts they read rather than to accept them passively. Torrance (*18*) suggests:

> Teachers can help children become creative readers in two major ways. First they can do things to help heighten the child's expectation and anticipation as a reading task is approached. Second they can permit or encourage children to do something with what is read, either at the time it is read or afterwards.

It has been the experience of this writer that the following procedures are helpful in promoting creative writing:

1. To provoke interest in creative reading from the start, a simple picture book story such as *May I Bring A Friend?* by Beatrice Shenk de Regniers (about a boy who was invited to tea by the king and queen) may be employed. This funny fantasy is an ideal vehicle for encouraging children to react creatively and imaginatively. In the story, the king and queen have told a boy to bring his friends to tea. The boy has many animal friends. Which friends shall he bring? Told in verse, this delightful story may be used to encourage children to anticipate and check various outcomes depending on the animals they choose to go to the party. They make suggestions from their own experiences, discuss outcomes, and check to determine the suitability of their choices as the progression of events is unfolded.

2. Another helpful way to promote thinking responses is by the use of an inventory which contains a number of questions addressed to children about their interests. Young children, almost without exception, will report activities such as watching TV programs, enjoying animals, and playing games of various kinds. The range will be extensive and varied. Common interests may be ascertained and extended through reading. A readily accessible avenue for further enrichment of interests is available through the film or filmstrip. For example, the film **Three Little Kittens** may be shown to primary grade children interested in pets; the film presentation may be halted after the exciting viewing of the newborn kittens. The children may then be asked to indicate what will happen now? What is to be done with the kittens? Thinking and speculation follow; finally the showing of the film is complete and the film reader (D.C. Heath) is examined to evaluate the accuracy and suitability of their guesses.

3. In history classes, sequences of events may be discussed in order, and at critical points the question "What do you think will happen now?" may be asked after the class has read a chapter silently to a place just preceding a significant happening (*18*). Books may be closed and a discussion of possibilities may proceed. Later, the reading of the chapter may be completed to ascertain what actually happened. Thus, we see how creative reading may be initially stimulated and motivated further during the reading process. Follow-up activities may assure elaboration or extension of what is read.

Follow-up Activities

One of the simplest and most effective follow-up activities to employ after silent reading is to have children **read aloud** exciting stories and poems they have enjoyed. Intonation, gesture, and movement may be used to reveal the child's pleasure, indignation, or surprise as he reads. The class or a particular child may retell a story and listen to it via tape or the magnetic sound track. Or a story may be retold in poetic form. Children may be encouraged to read materials with the thought in mind that they are to write a poem from a passage—or make a book report in varied forms. They may also dramatize a story or devise a puppet play from an exciting part of the book. A script for a movie, radio, or TV program may be prepared in which materials from a book or parts of it may be presented in a novel form.

Pupils may also extend and enrich their reading through the use of other media such as painting, singing, and dramatizing presentations. Writing a new ending for a story or completing an unfinished story are other ways of extending reading in creative forms (*18, 29*).

For example, the writer prepared for the *Highlights for Children* magazine a short story entitled "The Cat in the Wall" which was based on a newspaper account about a child's beloved cat that disappeared. After some time, the cat's whereabouts were revealed when her meows resounded from one of the dining room walls. Attempts were made, to no avail, to entice the cat to come out. At last, the fire department was called and a hole was cut in the wall. As the family watched to see the cat pulled out of the wall, there was a meow at the front door. The story was stopped at this point and children were asked to submit endings telling how the cat got in and out of the wall. Many elaborated ingeniously on what they had read and revealed their ability to think in unique and imaginative ways. As Torrance (*18*) states:

> For the gifted child, however, work in elaborating what is read will have its greatest usefulness in developing the ability to relate the content of reading to previous knowledge, produce illustrations and applications, practice using what has been read, relate what has been read to other fields, and make associations that integrate reading into action.

Personal Discovery and Application Through Reading

A good story may evoke questions and problems to be solved by additional reading. Thus, a gifted pupil was led to read and compare many long biographies of Thomas Jefferson after he had examined a provocative short story about Jefferson and his times. With the help of a librarian, he read widely about the varied accomplishments of this remarkable man. His discoveries caused him to make extensive personal plans and to remark, "Everyone should read about the many things this man did to make our country great. Each of us ought to be able to do something, especially when we realize what one man was able to do."

Another creative young reader was fascinated by a short biography of James Garfield and became a great admirer of this President who died at the hands of an assassin when he was very young. He sought to answer the question: What might this President have accomplished had he lived longer? This enticing topic was explored, and the boy composed a provocative essay in which he projected the life of this gifted President into a future wherein he made many important contributions to the finding of solutions to pressing social problems and issues.

Critical Reading and Evaluation

Evaluation of what is read is one of the chief features of creative reading. The creative reader often has a purpose or goal for reading which may be present when he starts to read to answer a particular question. A question may, of course, arise during or after his reading.

Reading as a thinking process often involves an effort to answer questions and solve problems, a process in which the pupil formulates an hypothesis and seeks to verify his conclusions.

Critical reading and creative reading are not always clearly differentiated. Critical reading is one aspect of creative reading; creative reading is, however, not always critical in nature. In reading a poem, a pupil may have an appreciative reaction, an emotional response which is largely uncritical in the usual sense. In such a case, the pupil may evaluate his response as to whether he experienced the joy or pleasure he anticipated and whether the response was sufficiently rewarding to cause him to seek further satisfaction from similar experiences. The critical reader may consider the author's background and competency for writing on the subject. He may also inquire about the author's freedom from bias and prejudice. Discovery of the limitations and prejudices of a writer may indeed become the chief goal of the pupil as he reads. Torrance (*18*) observes:

> Ferreting out the truth from what one reads requires that one be both a critical and a creative reader. Being a critical reader only makes a child aware of the biases and deficiencies in the accounts of writers. It takes a creative reader to understand the reasons behind discrepant accounts and reach sound conclusions about what is true.

The creative reader seeks sound conclusions, evaluates them, and makes valid decisions about their meaning and application.

PROGRAMS FOR CREATIVE READING

The writer believes that the experimental evidence from physiological and Gestalt psychology demonstrates children's capacity for insightful behavior and for thinking in early childhood. As a result of an examination of many studies, Russell (*12*) states:

> ...critical, creative reading is possible at all levels of the elementary school. Reasoning ability seems to begin at about three years of age and to develop gradually with experience and language. It develops continuously rather than appearing at fixed stages. There seems to be little difference in the way adults and children think, except that adults have a wider experience against which they may check their hypotheses and conclusions.

Gradually, school personnel are coming to accept the fact that children are capable of thinking and reasoning at early ages. Experiments have shown that insightful learning is possible in young children. Facts about children's learning during the early years (presented in books such as Maya Pines' *Revolution in Learning*) have caused many parents and teachers to recognize and accept the importance of cultivating intelligent response during the early years (*11*). Accordingly, creative reading programs are being initiated and the range and complexity of learning experiences are being extended for young children.

Advocates of creative reading are contributing to the improvement of instruction for junior-senior high school students by placing primary emphasis on reading as a part of a broad program in the humanities. For example, in Brockton, Massachusetts, **Ceiling Unlimited** is a unique project employing varied sources in the humanities organized around the central theme of man's understanding of himself (*1*). In other programs, solutions to broad social problems are sought.

A popular approach at the junior high school level is described by Barbe and Renzulli (*1*). Critical reading and thinking constitute the major objectives of this program developed by the Great Books Foundation. Through the use of carefully developed discussion questions and materials, each pupil from the third grade to the twelfth is encouraged to examine "the material in a way that is significant in terms of his own background, capacity, attitude, and interest."

Thus we see an increased interest in innovative programs for the gifted and the creative student as well as a greater tendency to foster creative reading in some schools. It is hoped that the future will see the expansion of such programs. Moreover, it is hoped that creative reading will be encouraged by teachers and practiced more frequently by students. For, as Toynbee (*20*) has written

> To give a fair chance to potential creativity is a matter of life and death for any society. This is all-important, because the outstanding creative ability of a fairly small percentage of the population is mankind's ultimate capital asset, and the only one with which only Man has been endowed.

SUMMARY

The gifted child is described according to traditional concepts based on early research which led to the designation of children of high IQ as gifted. The characteristics of such verbally gifted pupils are described. The creative pupil is also described in terms of recent research. Verbally gifted and creative pupils are then compared. It is shown that if a high IQ criterion is used to select the gifted, a majority of creative pupils might be missed. It is proposed that the gifted child be redefined as any pupil whose performance in a worthwhile type of human endeavor is consistently or repeatedly remarkable, thus making possible the inclusion of creative pupils in such areas as science and mathematics, music, art, writing, and social leadership. The validity of tests of creativity is also examined. It is proposed that the work-samples and other techniques in which pupils' gifts are judged by their performance be used more widely in selecting the gifted. Illustrations are given of specific ways to elicit evidence of giftedness.

Creative reading is recommended for gifted pupils. This highest type of reading is considered to be a thinking process in which new ideas are originated, evaluated, and applied. Divergent and varied responses, not right answers, are goals as thinking transpires and conclusions are reached. Finally, the pupil evaluates his conclusions and seeks to extend and use them. This concept is based upon the views presented by Torrance (*18*), Russell (*12*), and Jarolimek (*9*).

The presentation includes examples of ways the teacher may encourage creative reading in the classroom. Examples of programs to promote creative reading in our schools are also cited and creative reading and creative writing are viewed as parts of a desirable language arts approach for the gifted.

References

1. Barbe, Walter B., and Joseph Renzulli. "Innovative Programs for the Gifted and Creative," in Paul Witty (Ed.), *Reading for the Gifted and the Creative Student*. Newark, Delaware: International Reading Association, 1971.
2. Bloom, Benjamin S. et al. *Taxonomy of Educational Objectives*, Handbook I, Cognitive Domain. New York: Longmans-Green, 1956.
3. Bryan, J. Ned, and Lanora G. Lewis. "Are State Departments Failing to Provide for the Gifted?" *Accent on Talent*, 2 (May 1968).
4. DeBoer, John J. "Creative Reading and the Gifted Student," *Reading Teacher*, May 1963.
5. Durkin, Dolores. *Children Who Read Early*. New York: Teachers College Press, Columbia University, 1966.
6. Getzels, J. W., and P. W. Jackson. *Creativity and Intelligence*. New York: John Wiley and Sons, 1962.
7. Goertzel, Victor, and Mildred G. Goertzel. *Cradles of Eminence*. Boston: Little, Brown, 1962.
8. Guilford, J. P. "Potentiality for Creativity," *Gifted Child Quarterly*, 6 (Autumn 1962); "Structure of Intellect," *Psychological Bulletin*, 53 (1956).
9. Jarolimek, John. "The Taxonomy: Guide to Differentiated Instruction," *Social Education*, 25 (1962).
10. Jarolimek, John. "Skills Teaching in the Primary Grades," *Social Education*, 31 (1967).
11. Pines, Maya. *Revolution in Learning: The Years from Birth to Six*. New York: Harper and Row, 1967.

12. Russell, David. *Children Learn to Read* (2nd ed.). Boston: Ginn, 1961; *Children's Thinking*, Ginn, 1956.
13. Smith, Richard J. "Questions for Teachers—Creative Reading," *Reading Teacher,* February 1969. See also N. Sanders, *Classroom Questions—What Kinds?* New York: Harper and Row, 1966.
14. Taylor, Calvin W. "Be Talent Developers," *Today's Education*, 57 (December 1968); "The Highest Potentials of Man," *Gifted Child Quarterly*, 13 (1969).
15. Terman, Lewis M. "The Discovery and Encouragement of Exceptional Talent," *American Psychologist*, 9 (June 1954).
16. Terman, Lewis M., and Melita H. Oden. "The Stanford Studies of the Gifted," in Paul A. Witty (Ed.), *The Gifted Child*. Boston: D. C. Heath, 1951.
17. Torrance, E. Paul. "Explorations in Creative Thinking," *Education*, 81 (December 1960); "Are the Torrance Tests of Creative Thinking Biased Against or in Favor of Disadvantaged Groups?" *Gifted Child Quarterly*, Summer 1971.
18. Torrance, E. Paul. *Gifted Children in the Classroom*. New York: Macmillan, 1965.
19. Torrance, E. Paul. "Problems of Highly Creative Children," *Gifted Child Quarterly*, Summer 1961.
20. Toynbee, Arnold. "Is America Neglecting Her Creative Minority?" *Accent on Talent*, 2 (January 1968).
21. Witty, Paul A. (Ed.). *Reading for the Gifted and the Creative Student*. Newark, Delaware: International Reading Association, 1971.
22. Witty, Paul A. "Contribution to the IQ Controversy from the Study of Superior Deviates," *School and Society*, 5 (April 20, 1940).
23. Witty, Paul A. "The Use of Films in Stimulating Creative Expression and in Identifying Talented Pupils," *Elementary English*, October 1956.
24. Witty, Paul A. *Helping the Gifted Child*. Chicago: Science Research Associates, 1952. (Revised with Edith H. Grotberg, 1970.)
25. Witty, Paul A. "Reading for the Gifted," in J. Allen Figurel (Ed.), *Reading and Realism*, 1968 Proceedings, Volume 13, Part 1. Newark, Delaware: International Reading Association, 1969.
26. Witty, Paul A. "The Gifted Child in 1967," in John C. Gowan and E. Paul Torrance (Eds.), *Educating the Ablest*. Itasca, Illinois: F. E. Peacock, 1971.
27. Witty, Paul A. "The Education of the Gifted and the Creative in the U.S.A." *Gifted Child Quarterly*, Summer 1971.
28. Witty, Paul A. "Early Learning—A Crucial Issue," *Highlights for Teachers*, No. 13.
29. Witty, Paul A. "Fostering Creative Reading," *Highlights for Teachers*, No. 25.

INGREDIENTS OF A CREATIVE READING PROGRAM

Walter B. Barbe
Highlights for Children

Creative reading has not been given adequate attention by those concerned with how children learn. For this reason, it is important to examine those issues involved in developing a creative reading program.

Any discussion of creativity necessitates an examination of the terms frequently associated with it. For many years the label "gifted" was applied to children of high potential as well as those with high achievement. In more recent years, another aspect of human potential has come to be recognized as of equal importance to intelligence. This aspect has been labeled by many as "creative potential." The gifted child is viewed as one, in a school setting, who has either achieved at a level considerably above that of his age group or given evidence of a potential to do so.

The creative child, however, is one who is able to function in a manner different from that of the traditional and to produce or perform in new and innovated ways. Creativity implies that the individual is not limited to seeking solutions in the traditional ways which he may have been taught. Instead, he views problems as being solvable and is able to free himself from traditional bounds to seek solutions. While instruction may not produce giftedness, freedom to use the abilities which one has in ways other than traditional ones can result in creativity from each child in the classroom. If this freedom is provided, and if guidance is given, creative reading will result.

GOALS OF READING INSTRUCTION

In general, the goal of reading instruction is the development of permanent skills and interests in reading. To assume that acquiring necessary word attack skills is enough is to oversimplify the task. Being able to call off words, without understanding and appreciation, is an almost meaningless exercise; knowing fewer words, and understanding and appreciating those known, appears to be more valuable.

– The ultimate goal of reading instruction is to enable children to read for a variety of purposes (e.g., information, clarification, verification, pleasure, or escape). Beyond this, it is hoped that children will have the desire to read throughout their lives.

– The creative reader is concerned with both the process and the results of reading. Too often reading instruction is concerned solely with the process of reading or solely with the results of reading without realizing that both are of utmost importance. Interest in reading and enjoyment while reading are both parts of the process. Obtaining specific information is part of the result, as is completing a book for the purpose of being able to say one has read it. Creative reading is thus a complex endeavor involving both process and result.

For example, the dramatic and important book, *Bury My Heart at Wounded Knee*, is not one which many people say they have enjoyed reading. The process of reading this book is by no means enjoyable, but the reader is certain to say that he is glad he read it. This seeming dichotomy causes some people to become confused about what should be pleasurable. That there is little enjoyment in reading about the white man's role in overcoming the Indians does not lessen the satisfaction one has in gaining knowledge which is helpful in molding attitudes and behavior in future situations.

– Identification which occurs in the case of a book such as *Bury My Heart at Wounded Knee* indicates one of the values of creative reading. To identify with the white man in such a book is impossible if one is a white man. Even the reader who may begin making such an identification will transfer his identification to the Indian. The result, therefore, is to view the role of the Indian in an entirely different light, one of the outcomes of creative reading of utmost importance for the mature, intelligent reader.

– For creative reading to occur, encouragement and instruction must come early in the child's learning-to-read process. For the teacher to believe that creative reading will occur at some later date when the child has mastered all of the basic skills of reading is a misconception of how learning occurs.

– Kindergarten and first grade teachers need to be conscious of what creative reading is all about and to provide situations in which the child is rewarded for reading creatively. The instruction may be incidental in the early stages of reading instruction, but it should be planned and intentional throughout the elementary grades; it should be an inherent part of any reading program at the secondary school level.

RESOURCES AND MATERIALS

It is to be assumed that teachers will utilize all resources and materials available in their classrooms, school, and community in the total educational program of developing children. Reading series, trade books, subject matter textbooks, and audiovisual aids—all—are expected to be part of the total instructional program. Special attention is directed here to some elements found to be essential in a satisfactory program.

Libraries or Learning Centers

The library or learning center is the greatest asset which the teacher possesses in promoting creative reading. The teacher can hope to develop creative reading to its fullest only if there is an abundance of material from which children may select those things which they want to read. Merely aiming the child to materials is not enough; planned, intentional instruction in the art of reading creatively must occur.

Readily accessible materials are a first step. This means that every classroom should have a library of materials pertaining to particular subjects or special interests. A home library, the contents of which change as the child becomes older, is also to be encouraged.

In addition to classroom and home libraries, there is still the utmost need for the school library. But the school library must be more accessible than it has frequently been in the past. The library needs to be a center—not just for the bound book with the hard cover but also for paperbacks, current magazines, newspapers, and up-to-date reference books.

Materials

There are numerous sources of materials appropriate for promoting creative reading. The traditional type of unfinished story found frequently in *Highlights for Children* is one such example. The children are asked to provide an ending to a story which may have many different endings, none of which is the correct one, for there is no single correct ending.

The motivation to read further may come from free discussion about material which a number of children have read. Or, the discussion may cause some children to reread material in a creative manner after gaining more insight into the topic.

Best Books in Print (Bowker) is an extensive listing of materials for children to read, as are the books on the American Library Association's list. *A Parent's Guide to Children's Reading* and *Teacher's Guide to Children's Reading* by Nancy Larrick (Doubleday) are both musts for any teacher who is to encourage creative reading among children. **Reading Ladders to Human Understanding**, edited by Muriel Crosby (American Council on Education), groups books into categories around problems currently facing children. The use of this reference can more easily promote involvement and identification on the part of children than any other action.

Use of Biographies

It is a known fact that bright children turn early to biographies. Frequently as early as the second grade, children of high ability will begin to select biographies in an attempt to identify with success. They have essentially mastered the basic skills of knowing how to read, have acquired critical reading skills, and have begun to acquire creative reading skills which require both projection and identification. The most obvious identification, of course, is that which occurs in a biography when the reader views himself in the role of the main character who is ultimately successful. (One wonders whether the early introduction of biographies to children other than those of high ability might alter their self-concepts and their ultimate achievement.)

The teacher at any level must recognize the value of biographies. However, she must be cautioned against the selection of a single type, such as presidents of the United States. For identification to occur, the biography must be about a person with whom the child can *most* easily identify. There are presently more biographies of successful sports figures than ever before; these should be made available to children, along with other types of biographies.

Emphasizing the importance of identification to creative reading implies an issue on which there is currently much disagreement. It is apparent that many people do not believe that children are influenced in their behavior by what they read. If this is true, and the present writer vehemently disagrees, then there seems to be little basis for a belief in creative reading. On the other hand, if children are influenced by what they read, then creative reading is indeed important in the development of self-concept, the establishment of lifestyle, and ultimate success in assuming a responsible role in society. So that there is no misunderstanding, let me repeat that it is this writer's strong belief that the printed word influences behavior. Believing this, the selection of material for children to read then becomes of utmost importance. Creative reading, as discussed here, becomes more than merely reading beyond what the author intended; it actually becomes an element in the character and goal-setting development of each child.

REQUIRED SKILLS

Creative Reading Skills

Creative reading is the highest level of reading—higher even than critical reading. It is supposed by some that reading cannot be creative, for the reader is limited by the thoughts and words of the author. This is untrue; the person who brings his own background and experiences to reading may then take from the reading selection far more than the author intended. An understanding of the author's motivation for writing a particular piece, and knowledge about the author's background and the circumstances in which the selection was written, aid the reader in interpreting the material and also in achieving a unique view of a situation or an event as he integrates his and the author's experiences. To limit one's self to merely the literal meaning of the words which the author chose to use, or even to inferred meanings based on knowledge of the author's intentions, is to attain far less understanding than can result from creative thinking about what is read.

Creative reading cannot exist without the presence of confidence in one's ability to read and understand the author's meaning; it also requires analysis, synthesis, and evaluation abilities associated with critical reading.

Teachers must be concerned with more than just traditional skills or traditional reading materials. Basal programs provide for a sequential development of skills, and the materials lend themselves to certain types of thinking activities which will promote creative reading; however, the possibilities are limited, and a wide range of other materials and resources are required to meet the needs of particular children at particular times.

Each individual has particular books which have somehow changed his life. This very change was possible because of what the reader brought to the book; not solely what the author put into the book as has sometimes been thought.

Certain books do better lend themselves to creative reading at certain age levels because of their content and the author's writing skill. Teachers should always be on the lookout for such books. Perhaps the classic example for third grade children is *Charlotte's Web* by E. B. White. In this amazing book, a child encounters new concepts for the first time and his reactions are inherently creative for the child responds in terms of his own unique makeup and not in some predetermined way.

The novel, *Burr*, by Gore Vidal has been used successfully to promote creative reading with gifted high school students. One technique is to challenge the reader by the statement: "From this book I learned more about Gore Vidal than I did about Aaron Burr."

Listening and Viewing Skills

The use of films, filmstrips, recordings, photographs, and television programs must be promoted; training in all of the listening and viewing skills should be part of the program. Only if the child views all of the many audiovisual materials available to him as aids to his creative reading can he be freed from the concept of reading as a limited activity confined to content found between the two covers of a single book.

Library Skills

Library skills are among the many skills needing further attention. This does not mean the traditional type of instruction which requires children to learn only how to locate different kinds of materials. Children must discover how to locate the names of important authors, facts about their lives, and sources where they can find out more about such people. They must be led to utilize many types of reference materials, make comparisons from a variety of sources, and understand the processes involved in locating various kinds of information. The advanced library skills will be learned easily and happily by children who have problems to solve, needs to meet, and interests to follow.

Recording Skills

Just as knowing how to find material is important, so is the ability to record what one wishes to express. Handwriting is an essential skill, and being able to write rapidly and legibly is important. Knowing how to use a typewriter is another valuable skill; there can be little justification for delaying instruction in the use of a typewriter much past the point of the child's attainment of writing abilities.

Notetaking and outlining skills must be developed within a framework of problem-solving. As children have a need to organize their ideas, they will have a need to learn shortcuts in producing written records. In some instances, they may need or want to learn minimal shorthand skills.

Creative Writing Skills

Creative reading and creative writing cannot be separated, for creative reading is dependent upon the child's ability to organize his

A Creative Reading Program

creative interpretations and either record or report them. This is impossible if the child is limited to rigid forms and to traditional reciting of facts. It is likely that creative writing instruction will precede high-level creative reading. The mechanical aspects of reproducing one's thoughts must be minimized, as well as the importance of spelling and legible penmanship, as a child first grapples with the problems of expressing his thoughts. With practice and experiences of various types, the child may acquire an automaticity that will enable him to produce a final product that will meet the standards of good reporting.

The very young child draws pictures to which he gives labels. Later, he labels his own pictures; then, he wants complete sentences. At each step, he depends upon someone more capable to record his thoughts. When he has mastered handwriting skills, he can copy what others wrote as he dictated; soon, he can write for himself. There will be a period of time for the gifted and creative child when he will have thinking and oral language abilities far ahead of his written language skills. It is essential that teachers enable such children to have the assistance needed to record their ideas without being penalized for lacking spelling skills, or for tiring quickly from holding a pencil.

If teachers can view creative writing in much the same way that they view drawings or constructions, they will realize that children need freedom to express themselves without fear of criticism, no matter what form of expression is used. At the same time, as teachers provide instruction in basic skills, they will note both progress and problems, resulting in rewards for successes and renewed efforts to master skills.

For the child to be able to write creatively, he must be able to think creatively. And when he can think creatively he can also read creatively. Creative thinking is most certainly the basis for both creative writing and creative reading.

SUMMARY

The goal of reading instruction must extend beyond the mere acquisition of the skill of reading. The ultimate goal must be involvement in the process of reading which results in creative reading and writing. To the extent that we aid children in going beyond merely learning how to read we are fulfilling our roles as creative teachers.

PART TWO

SPECIAL CONSIDERATIONS

Breaking down barriers to fostering creative reading requires *clarification of problems* and *recommendations for meeting needs*. This section deals with special aspects that must be considered when developing reading programs for gifted and creative learners.

As education moves more and more toward individualization in one way or another, teachers and parents must seek additional ways to meet individual needs, to innovate, to utilize creative teaching strategies, and to provide for all levels of learners. A vast amount of theoretically sound current information has been presented. The content is valuable to parents and teachers concerned with fostering creative reading at all levels.

The comments concerning home and parent involvement should enable teachers to consider realistically the reasons why some parents have not assumed an adequate role early in their children's lives. Moreover, the ideas presented should motivate teachers to involve parents at later periods so that there is more help given by all people involved in the academic education of gifted and creative learners. Principals and teachers are provided guidance for developing programs of Early Childhood Education and later grades which offer genuine help to talented learners in all stages of their thinking and reading growth.

M.L.

PARENT ROLES IN FOSTERING READING

Edith H. Grotberg
The American University

Parents are particularly important in the development of their gifted and creative children and the need for schools to work with these parents is increasingly clear. Studies repeatedly show the role of parents as they provide a home background conducive to the development of their children, as they interact with the school in a variety of relationships, and as they help their children develop their gifts and talents on a continuing basis.

THE HOMES OF GIFTED AND CREATIVE CHILDREN

One method for determining what factors are critical to the development of gifted and creative children is to study the homes of both gifted and nongifted children to isolate those things that differentiate the homes. What is present in the homes of the gifted that is absent in the homes of the nongifted? What do parents of the gifted do that is not done by parents of the nongifted? What is the effect of socioeconomic level on home characteristics for differentiating gifted and nongifted children? Some of the most important research directed to answering these questions has been done by Ira Gordon and Robert Hess. Further significant studies have been conducted in other countries but have relevance to the United States.

Gordon (1), in his own research and in reviewing the research of others, identified a total of nineteen factors in parent behavior which are related to child performance. Not only is the presence of these factors important to child performance, but of importance also are the degrees to which these factors operate. Of the nineteen critical factors, nine are cognitive or intellectual and ten are emotional or affective. The cognitive factors are as follows:

1. *Academic guidance*. The parents interest their children in learning and exploring activities and encourage them to ask questions and seek answers. They encourage their children to take the initiative and praise them for their efforts.

2. *Cognitive operational level and style.* The parents encourage their children to reason and solve problems and test their ideas with actions. The parents use this cognitive style themselves and provide a model of approach and style.
3. *Cultural activities planned.* The parents structure plans for their children to have cultural experiences and expose them to a large variety of such activities. "Let's go to the zoo." "Let's attend the children's concert." "Let's watch this television show." These are some of the planning strategies.
4. *Direct instruction of the child.* The parents teach their children how to do a task, how to solve a problem, how to make choices, and how to assess results. In addition, the parents observe their children as they are learning and offer appropriate suggestions and encouragements.
5. *Educational aspirations.* The parents place high value on education and either actively encourage their children to participate in educational activities and goals or simply assume the children will place value on education because they themselves do. This is generally a valid assumption.
6. *Use of external resources.* The parents have their children attend nursery school or kindergarten or they may place them in special summer activity programs, such as day camp. Many children learn to love books not only because their parents tend to love books but also because their parents have encouraged them to participate in "the children's hour" at many libraries.
7. *Intellectuality of the homes.* The parents have books and magazines around the home and usually have dictionaries and encyclopedias. The parents are seen reading these books and using them as references. They are also heard discussing what they have read.
8. *Verbal facility.* The parents use their vocabularies effectively to help their children learn. They do not need large or elaborate vocabularies; they need to use them to clarify expectations and guide progress.
9. *Verbal frequency.* The parents engage their children in conversation during mealtime or on car trips or at family gatherings. There is more use of words and universal language than nonverbal signals and contextual language.

Children need not only cognitive stimulation from their parents but also emotional support if their gifts and talents are to reach fruition. Gordon identified the following ten emotional factors in parent bahavior which are related to child performance:

1. *Consistency of management.* The parents maintain a consistent and, therefore, predictable style of management or discipline so that the children know what is expected of them and what kinds of limits are clearly established. There are no shocking surprises or uncertainties.
2. *Differentiation of self.* The parents do not confuse themselves with their children. They know where their personality ends and another's begins.
3. *Disciplinary pattern.* The parents behave in their own lives with a sense of self-discipline and an expression of this in their daily performance. The children accept patterns of behavior expressive of this discipline and imitate the models.
4. *Emotional security, self-esteem.* The parents feel safe and loved and respect themselves as significant individuals. They thus have emotional energy available to provide emotional security to their children and opportunities for the children to develop self-esteem.
5. *Impulsivity.* The parents do not engage in erratic, unpredictable behavior, but rather have their behavior under some rational control without repressing creative thoughts and feelings.
6. *Belief in internal control.* The parents stress the importance of building internal controls rather than relying on external controls. Closely allied to this is the belief in assuming responsibility for their own behavior.
7. *Protectiveness, babying of child.* The parents recognize the dependency of their children and are willing to permit them to act out that dependency. The parents provide the protective, nurturing behavior necessary for children to feel protected.
8. *Trusting attitude.* The parents trust each other and trust their children. They encourage their children to trust others and to be receptive to learning experiences others might provide. Children who distrust others learn in a distorted way.
9. *Willingness to devote time to the children.* The parents plan activities for their children and enjoy spending time carrying out these activities. Parents need to communicate their pleasure in spending time with their children.
10. *Work habits.* The parents demonstrate to their children that they have developed work habits which permit the

acceptance and completion of an activity. The parents also place value on a high level of performance and quality work. They, in effect, respect what they do.

Hess (*6*), identified nine categories of parent behavior which influence child development: 1) independence training, 2) warmth and high emotional involvement, 3) consistency of discipline, 4) explanatory control, 5) expectation for success, 6) parents' sense of control, 7) the verbalness in the home, 8) parents' direct teaching, and 9) parental self-esteem.

A number of studies of infants support the contention that parents influence the development of their children.

The Illinois study (*13*), found several items which consistently related to child cognitive performance in the first two years of life: "There was at least one magazine placed where the child could play with it or look at it; the child was given regular training in one or more skills; the mother spontaneously vocalized to the child; the mother spontaneously named at least one object to the child while the observer was in the home; the father helped take care of the child; the father played with the child at least ten minutes a day; the child was regularly spoken to by parents during mealtimes."

Miller (*10*), in reviewing the research on the relationships between family variables and scholastic performance in English schools, lists the following as positively related to school performance: "homes where independent thinking and freedom of discussion occur, where there are values conducive to intellectual effort, where children's curiosity and academic aspirations are supported, and in which there is harmony between home and school values."

Keeves (*7*), in an extensive study of children in the Australian capitol territory, uncovered relationships of early adolescents between school performance and home environment. He reported that "... the importance of the mother's attitudes and ambitions stands out quite clearly, but are exceeded in importance by the provision made in the home for stimulation to learn and to promote intellectual development." In a study in Utrecht, Holland, Rupp (*11*) indicated the "cultural-pedagogical aspects of upbringing" and found that, when high achievers were compared with low achievers within the lowest socioeconomic class, the high achievers came from homes in which parents held this cultural-pedagogical point of view. They saw themselves as educators. They practiced this by "... reading to their children, playing table games and word games with them, providing educational toys and books, reading and possessing books themselves, telling their children informative things of their own accord, teaching their children preschool skills, going to places of interest."

It is important to note how frequently emotional factors are identified as critical to promoting gifts and talents in children. Not only do parents help their children more when they themselves have a good sense of who they are, a feeling of stability and emotional security, and a sense of control and worth, but they also need to be supportive and encouraging of their children. Patterns of parental indifference, rejection, or oversolicitude impair the children's development and may crush their talents. One expression of this turmoil is underachievement (*3, 4*).

The assumption that gifted and creative children come only from advantaged homes or higher-income homes is questionable. In earlier studies, from Terman (*12*) to Martinson (*9*), reports are clear that gifted and creative children emerge from a cross section of the socioeconomic spectrum.

In a careful review of the research on the effect of socioeconomic level of the home on the development of the child, Gordon (*1*) found some evidence that middle-income parents tended to have more effective techniques with their children than low-income parents. He cautioned, however, that his research, as well as that of Hess and Shipman (*5*), White (*15*), and Watts (*14*), indicates there is tremendous variability within social class groups. Gordon states: "If we are interested in identifying particular parental attributes which we feel are desirable, then social class is not a usable label. . . . Our infant research all clearly indicates that the amount of conversation in the home, particularly the *amount* directed toward the child, relates significantly to child performance."

PARENTS AS TEACHERS

Parents provide an environment in which their children are totally immersed. Most early childhood experiences are within a parent-determined environment, but parents are generally unaware that they are performing as teachers. Parents need to be made aware of their role as teachers and then to acquire teaching skills to enhance the development of their children. Research describes how parents, once aware of their role, affect the learning of their children. Teaching includes setting the stage for learning, modeling, managing the environment, giving information, and engaging in direct interaction. These components of teaching are incorporated in numerous research studies. The research findings relate to the effects on children of programs which focus heavily on training the parents as teachers and programs which focus heavily on teaching the child with some parent involvement as teachers.

Virtually all of the recent and current research relating to parents as teachers focuses on low-income parents and their children. Those few studies which include middle-income and mixed socioeconomic groups use these groups mainly for comparison purposes. Almost without exception, the parent involved is the mother. Few fathers have participated in these programs; those who have are apt to have participated either in decision-making positions or in programs designed to increase the skill of the father for his own development.

SPECIAL PROGRAMS

Training Parents as Teachers

Programs which are largely parent-oriented include using television as a media of instruction, training parents to work in the home with their children, and training parents through group discussion techniques.

In almost all of the studies in which mothers are trained to be tutors of their own children in their homes, the children show greater immediate gains in intellectual, conceptual, or language development. These findings occur in projects involving home visits only, in preschool projects operated in the home, in preschool plus home visiting projects, and in projects in which the mothers are trained to work at home with their children but receive few, if any, home visits. Lazar and Chapman (8), report that in four studies parent-teaching with or without a preschool component resulted in greater immediate effect on children's language, intellectual, or academic achievement than a preschool program only. In one project concerned with infants younger than one year of age, superiority of the experimental group of children was not maintained at age two if parent-teaching was terminated at age one, but it was maintained if parent teaching continued until the child reached age two.

Though relatively few studies have included a follow up of these home teaching programs, those which did usually reported that gains continued to be apparent. In two projects having only a home visit and introducing parent-teaching after age one, intellectual levels remained significantly above or at the initial testing. In two projects involving preschool plus home visits, experimental group children showed beneficial effects upon entering school and through the middle primary grades without further parent-teaching.

The few results available on the impact of parent-teaching in association with mass-media child development efforts suggest that parent encouragement and parent-child activities associated with educational television programs for young children may enhance the cognitive gains made by the children as a result of the television program.

Though difficult, it is possible to engage a sizeable proportion of low-income mothers of preschool children in groups to discuss concerns about themselves, their communities, and their children. A number of studies have reported that the skill and sensitivity of the group leader or trainer is crucial in getting the attendance of the parents and in subsequently engaging them in active participation in the group. While those parents who attend such groups represent a self-selected population which no doubt differs from the non-attending parents, those who do attend generally express positive feelings about the effect of the group experience on themselves and on the behavior of their children. A number of studies have reported greater success in gaining attendance and participation of mothers when the content of the program was specific, such as language development, rather than sensitivity training or general discussions of child development. Two studies have reported greater immediate gains on the tests utilized for the children when the mothers took part in a structural language curricula, than when other types of discussion groups were utilized. Follow up on most studies has been lacking.

Partial Involvement of Parents as Teachers

These programs focus primarily on the child, while the parent component is of secondary or even incidental emphasis. Even among these studies, however, children in a preschool program tend to show greater immediate mean gains in IQ and achievement when their parents participate in a parent educational component aimed at increasing cognitive development. Other studies report no significant differences among the groups of children but have found some differences in attitude among the mothers. Some studies have reported greater group gains among mothers and children when the mothers have participated in a specific language training program to augment the program of their children, than when mothers take part in other group activities. One study indicates the possibility of "sleeper" effects in that attitude change among the mothers in the experimental group during the first year was not reflected in difference between groups of children until a later follow up. A number of ongoing and completed studies are attempting to bring about changes in mother-child interaction through behavior modification techniques which would supplement the program focusing primarily on the child.

In summary, most of the studies which have focused on training mothers as teachers of their children report positive immediate effects on the intellectual achievement or language development of the children. Studies which have provided a parent-teaching component as an adjunct to an ongoing children's program also show positive changes among the children but not with the same frequency as when parents are the primary focus of the training. These studies, however, concern young children and their parents. Very little has been done to study the effects on older children of parent-teaching activities. And yet children should benefit from parent-teaching experiences at any age.

The alert parents, for example, who know their children have learned how to read maps in school may well involve their children in planning a family trip. The maps are studied to determine route, road conditions, stopping places, and time involved. Parents do not need special training for this kind of activity, but they do need to be made aware of the skills their children have acquired and the uses to which they might be applied.

The concerned teachers at grades three, seven, or eleven may send home a book list for suggested birthday or Christmas gifts for children. The teacher may also encourage the children to involve their parents in research projects, particularly where reading is involved. The teacher may find the parents so interested that they seek a closer relationship with the teacher in order to further enhance the development of gifts and talents in their children.

It is easy for teachers to assume that parents who have not expressed an interest in helping their children do not wish to help them. The fact might well be that parents believe they are not to "interfere" with the education of their children, particularly as they move into higher grades. Further, parents who do not perceive their parent-teaching capability may appreciate some guidance from teachers. Teachers surely have an obligation to determine at any grade what parents might do to help their gifted children. And teachers have the knowledge and skills to show parents how to become involved in the development of their gifted and talented children.

HOME/SCHOOL RELATIONSHIPS

Homes cannot become schools any more than schools can become homes. They have unique functions which need to be maintained and respected. Nor can there be an unrestricted open-door policy. Schools should not tolerate an unannounced invasion by parents any more than homes should tolerate the unannounced home visit by teachers. The two institutions need some clear areas of separate autonomy. Respecting the uniqueness of each institution, there nevertheless remain large areas of interface or cooperation, and it is to these areas that we must address ourselves if we want our gifted and talented children to fulfill themselves. The interaction between home and school may take place in the home, in the school or preschool, or in a neighborhood learning center. Evidence has already been provided from the research literature that such interactions benefit children, but the research has not exhausted the possible ways of home/school cooperation nor has it generally addressed itself to home/school cooperation where older children are concerned. The recommendations presented here are partially based on research evidence but attempt to go beyond that evidence to what seem to be appropriate additional recommendations based on observation and experience.

1. *Bring the school to the home.* The expertise of the school is in learning-teaching. The school has materials, curricula, and a vast array of ideas and skills addressing themselves to the learning-teaching phenomenon. The school may bring these materials, ideas, and skills into the home through a home visitor, a resource teacher, or a mobile unit. School personnel may demonstrate activities in the home, leave materials on a lend-lease basis, or leave materials appropriate for a television show. The parents may ask questions, report progress, and indeed demonstrate their skills with their children.

   As children advance in school, they themselves can bring home materials and activities to use with their parents for the insights and assistance to be derived from their parents. Homework is the activity generally brought home and this seems to be designed to separate students from parents rather than have students benefit from the knowledge of their parents. Older children might bring home materials for their younger brothers and sisters and enjoy the experience of teaching them, reading to them, or engaging in some learning activity with them.

2. *Bring the home to the school.* Parents should be able to use the school facilities for a number of purposes to help their children.

   a. Use the library. Schools need to include library materials directed to parents who wish to select books to read for deeper understanding of their children, to read to their children, or to learn how to do things with their children. The International Reading Association published a helpful guide, *Reading for the Gifted and the Creative Student*, edited by Paul Witty.

   b. Have their children screened. Many promising children are handicapped by perceptual problems and learning difficulties. Parents take their children to medical doctors for health problems and to dentists for dental problems. Teachers should provide preschool as well as in-school screening to identify learning problems.

Screening for talent is also an important service the school might provide. Talents and gifts need nurturing from early childhood and many parents either do not recognize the gifts of their children or do not know what they can do to help their children. Some schools are already providing early screening services and guiding parents in readings and activities to enhance the talents of their children.

c. Observe classroom activities. Parents who watch their children functioning in a classroom are able to learn a great deal about how children's learning is enhanced. Indeed, with some guidance from the teachers, the parents may supplement classroom activities in order to reinforce the learning experiences. Often it is the dichotomy between home and school that presents problems to children.

d. Attend cultural activities. The school needs to be a cultural center for families. When children perform in plays, play an instrument in the orchestra, or have an art exhibit, both they and their parents may share a cultural activity. Some schools involve parents in organizing and planning for cultural activities.

3. *Establish community learning centers.* As an alternative to the home or the school being the locus for home/school cooperation, a community learning center has been suggested. This concept emerges from the increased awareness that the whole child, and not just his cognitive development, must be the focus of our attention if the child is to develop to his fullest. A community learning center might have materials on health and physical well-being; it might have a pediatrician, a psychologist, and an educator. Parents would bring their children to the center for diagnosis and screening to identify problems and to determine gifts and talents. At the same center, the parents might be provided with materials, books, and guidance in using them with their children. The entire family could attend activities together in the evening or on weekends and extend the children's learning experiences in a larger social community.

Many of these recommendations are in operation or are in the process of being implemented. All of the services must, of course, be used at the option of the parents.

But there seems little risk that such services will not be used. Parents have become extremely sensitive to their role in enhancing the development of their children, to the need for early identification and stimulation of gifts and talents, and to the need to look to schools and other community resources to help them. The school may lag behind parents in these understandings and may need some prodding from the parents. For the sake of the gifts and talents of their children, let them prod.

SUMMARY

Parents are the first educators of their children and are the first to be in a position to recognize unusual or remarkable abilities in their children. The research documents the effects of parent involvement and interaction with their children. The children are clearly helped or hindered in their development by the nature and quality of parent involvement. The importance of engaging in activities together, of talking together, of reading together—and for children to hear their parents read to them—is stressed over and over.

Teachers do not generally become involved with the education of children until after much learning has already occurred. It is important, then, for teachers to coordinate their efforts with what parents have already accomplished and to perceive the school/home relationship as a cooperative venture for the benefit of the development of children. This cooperation may begin at any time during the school years if early efforts were overlooked.

References

1. Gordon, I. R. *Parent Involvement in Compensatory Education.* Urbana, Illinois: University of Illinois Press, 1970.
2. Gordon, I. R. "What Do We Know About Parents-as-Teachers?" paper presented at the American Educational Research Association Convention, 1972.
3. Gowan, John C. "The Underachieving Gifted Child: A Problem for Everyone," *Exceptional Children*, 21 (April 1955), 247-249.
4. Grotberg, Edith H. "Adjustment Problems of the Gifted," *Education*, 82 (April 1962), 474-476.
5. Hess, R. D., and V. Shipman. "Cognitive Elements in Maternal Behavior," in J. P. Hill (Ed.), *Minnesota Symposia on Child Psychology*, Volume I. Minneapolis: University of Minnesota Press, 1967.
6. Hess, R. D. "Community Involvement in Day Care," in Edith H. Grotberg (Ed.), *Day Care: Resources for Decisions.* Office of Economic Opportunity, 1971.
7. Keeves, J. P. "The Home Environment and Educational Achievement," unpublished manuscript, Australian-National University, 1970.

8. Lazar, Joyce B., and Judith Chapman. *A Review of the Present Status and Future Research Needs of Programs to Develop Parenting Skills*, prepared for the Interagency Panel on Early Childhood Research and Development. Washington, D.C.: George Washington University, 1972.
9. Martinson, Ruth. *Educational Programs for Gifted Pupils*. Sacramento: California State Department of Education, 1961.
10. Miller, G. W. *Educational Opportunity and the Home*. London, England: Longman, 1971.
11. Rupp, J. C. C. *Helping the Child to Cope with School*. Groninger, Netherlands: Wolters-Noodhoff, 1969.
12. Terman, L. M. *Genetic Studies of Genius*. Stanford, California: Stanford University Press, 1925-1959.
13. Wachs, T. D., I. C. Uzgiris, and J. McV. Hunt. "Cognitive Development in Infants of Different Age Levels and from Different Environmental Backgrounds: An Exploratory Investigation," *Merrill-Palmer Quarterly*, 17 (1971), 283-317.
14. Watts, J. C., and J. C. Barnett. "Environment," mimeo manuscript, 1971.
15. White, B. L. "Fundamental Early Environmental Influences on the Development of Competency," in M. Meyer (Ed.), *Third Symposium On Learning: Cognitive Learning*. Bellingham, Washington: Western Washington State College, 1972.

LANGUAGE PROGRAMS FOR YOUNG CHILDREN: IMPLICATIONS FOR THE CREATIVE AND GIFTED

Dorothy S. Strickland
Kean College of New Jersey

The kind of education which a child receives in an early childhood program is largely determined by the philosophy of those who develop that program. This philosophy helps shape the curriculum, sets the tone for the overall learning environment, and ultimately determines the type of materials which are available to the child.

CURRENT PHILOSOPHICAL VIEWS

One of the major current philosophical conflicts facing early childhood educators today is focused on preschool or pre-first grade experience. This conflict holds far reaching implications for the creative and gifted child. Elkind ([1]) sees it as a "battle between the traditional middle-class nursery school teachers who see preschool education as development from within and the new breed of pre-school workers who see education as enforcement from without." In its extreme form, the conflict exists between those who hold that the purpose of preschool education is to enrich the life of the young child through a program entirely focused on social development and their opponents who place major emphasis on the direct instruction of specific skills and behaviors they consider important for success in school.

DETERMINING GOALS

Of course, few programs actually reflect such extremes in philosophy. Out of this very conflict, however, come a number of basic issues which early childhood teachers face as they plan for the children in their charge. On the one hand, most teachers would agree that socialization and self-expression should receive heavy emphasis in their programs. They recognize that readiness is a phenomenon which is determined primarily by each individual child's own rate of development; therefore, they would avoid academic pressure. At the same time, these teachers are faced with the equally important need to provide challenging cognitive experiences which will allow young children varied opportunities to acquire information and skills. The problem of providing academic stimulation without academic pressure lies at the heart of planning programs for all children in early childhood settings. Planning for gifted and creative children, however, requires special care to set goals which demand a balanced program.

In terms of reading, or perhaps we should say language experiences at this level, early childhood teachers are faced with many decisions. They must decide how much, if any, time will be given to the direct instruction of a set of specific skills. If direct instruction is to be given, it must be decided what content is to be included and what method of classroom organization will be most helpful. Thus, the question to be resolved is what combination of whole-group instruction, small-group instruction, and individualized instruction should be used. If no direct instruction is to be given, another question to be resolved is whether reliance on incidental learning will be sufficient to meet the goals of the program.

Teachers must make decisions about how they will view cognitive development. Will it be viewed in terms of the content mastered or in terms of the process involved? For reading, this may mean the difference between a program that emphasizes heavily the recognition of letters and words as opposed to a program which places as much or more importance on affective learnings such as creative drama and the enjoyment of literature.

Another important question to be faced by the early childhood teacher is whether his responsibility is primarily that of preparation for the future or planning for present needs. Whether to focus language arts experiences toward a goal of getting the children ready for some future grade or level, or to base those experiences on the assessment of the current needs and interests of the children for use as an avenue for language growth, is a critical decision.

PROGRAM PLANNING

The kinds of materials found in an early childhood classroom will reflect the manner in which the person who is responsible for that program has chosen to answer the questions raised above. In the interest of all children, but especially the gifted and creative, let us hope that the teacher faced with these choices will decide in favor of a total language arts program with clearly defined goals which relate primarily to individuals rather than to the group.

In addition, although most programs include varying amounts of direct instruction, undirected learning through a wide variety of materials should also be heavily relied upon. Broad goals should be set for the entire group, but major attention should be given to setting goals and expectations which are deliberately different for each child. The materials in such a program would necessarily provide for a wide range of abilities and capabilities.

Cognitive development should be viewed in terms of process rather than product, allowing for a broad range of activities rather than a narrow program designed to promote a set of specific skills. The use of drama, music, art, and movement would become a significant part of the language arts program. The process of making one's own materials would be an extremely important experience for the child. Thus, commercially prepared materials, teacher-made materials, and materials prepared by the students would all receive status in the program.

Let us also hope that these teachers will decide against a language program which focuses entirely on getting children ready for some future grade or level. When future accomplishment is the main concern of the language arts program, the reading curriculum tends to be relatively fixed and little flexibility is allowed for individual differences. Planning for present needs allows for a wide range of learning opportunities which enable the child to progress as rapidly as his interest and ability will allow.

There should be an adequate, continual assessment of abilities for all children. For gifted and creative children, there would then be an early identification of talent and superior potential. Early identification is important for both the child who learns to read before formal instruction normally begins and for the child who does not learn to read early but who needs to be encouraged to move ahead to more advanced work as soon as he has a need or a desire.

The program would set no minimum standards of achievement for all children, since such standards generally become the norm for the entire group and therefore may be too optimistic for the slow child and too limiting for the gifted child. The materials in such a program would provide for the broad range of differences within the group. It is quite possible and desirable that everything, from blocks and beads to reading materials and dictionaries, would be found in the same classroom. Moreover, all children may use the entire range of materials as needs arise.

SELECTING MATERIALS

When considering materials, the teacher's first responsibility is to insure a stimulating room environment. Just as the housekeeping corner, the block area, and the art center are valuable in an early childhood program, a language arts center should also be part of that program. This area would be a place where children go to read and to write.

For reading, the center should be equipped with picture books, picture story books, easy readers, and books made by the teacher and by the children. Experience charts and stories should be hung on walls or on easels. A list of the children's names should be available for their use; magazines, puzzles, and language games should also be available.

For writing, there should be sufficient pencils, crayons, magic markers, and other types of writing materials available. Plenty of paper in all sizes, shapes, and colors should be ready and waiting for use by the children. A primary typewriter should also be there for typing one's name or a note or a list or just for the fun of finding the letters one knows.

The literature collection in such a classroom should be both broad and varied. It will go beyond the usual collection of ABC, counting, nursery rhyme, poetry, nature, and story books to include a large assortment of easy reading material. Heavy emphasis should be placed on concept books dealing with a variety of abstract ideas. Catalogs and old magazines should be on hand for use as picture resources or for browsing. Children's magazines and reference materials should be available. Gifted and creative children are especially curious during these early years and require many resources for the answers to their constant questioning; teachers can expect gifted and creative children to make frequent use of dictionaries, encyclopedias, and other resource materials with the help of the teacher, other adults, and older children.

A collection of pictures, classified and filed according to subject and/or use, can be an invaluable aid to the early childhood teacher. Such pictures may be used as stimulators for discussion, storytelling, role playing, and vocabulary building activities. Small pictures may be used for classification exercises.

An assortment of audiovisual materials should also be included in a well-equipped early childhood classroom. A record player for listening to stories, music, and poetry is important. A tape recorder will provide endless hours of enjoyable and purposeful activity. Children especially enjoy reading original stories based on textless picture storybooks. A puppet theater and puppets may be used for creative dramatics. A flannel board may be used in a number of ways, including classifying information and retelling stories while putting cutouts in proper sequence.

SUMMARY

The early years require a flexible program for children if they are to be guided toward maximum achievement and the expression of talent. An early childhood program that recognizes this will be staffed with teachers who, because they are knowledgeable about the characteristics of young gifted and creative students, will insure their early identification. Such a program will provide support and motivation for these children, allowing them to progress as fast and as far as their interests and abilities will allow. The language arts curriculum will provide a broad range of experiences for all children so that those who exhibit early reading potential may receive the freedom to learn to read with complete support and encouragement. Most important, the language arts program will provide abundant opportunities for all children to participate in a variety of intellectually stimulating activities. This is essential if young children are to develop their full potential for successful learning.

Reference

1. Elkind, David. "Preschool Education: Enrichment or Instruction?" *Childhood Education*, 45 (February 1969), 321-328.

USING READING TO STIMULATE CREATIVE
THINKING IN THE INTERMEDIATE GRADES

Richard J. Smith
University of Wisconsin at Madison

In *The Prophet*, Gibran (*4*) writes that if a teacher "... is indeed wise, he does not bid you enter the house of his wisdom, but rather leads you to the threshold of your own mind." As a vehicle for taking students to the thresholds of their own minds, reading has few equals. Torrance (*12*) says, "A good story, biography, or other reading material is likely to evoke many ideas and questions which can send the reader far beyond what is read." Students who do not develop the habit of reading beyond the lines miss the many pleasant intellectual excursions they might take while reading.

Consider the following passage from *The Comback Guy* (*3*): "Once more he visualized himself standing, pole poised, at the end of the runway. Down the runway, high in the sky above the pit, the crossbar swayed gently, challenging him and mocking him." The student who pauses to see, in his mind's eye, Jeff's vaulting over the bar or twisting his ankle, and to hear the words of praise or sighs of disappointment from Jeff's schoolmates, has taken advantage of some of the thinking potential in the story. Another student reading the same passage might pause briefly to recall the time he himself stood at home plate with two strikes and the winning run on third. He might form in his mind the words, "Do it, Jeff," as he supplies the colors, the sounds, and the smells the author didn't describe when he wrote the story. Readers who make these kinds of additions to the material they read are creative readers.

Creative reading is an elusive concept, and different people who write about the phenomenon may conceptualize it differently. Perhaps Johnson (*5*) comes close to the conceptualization offered in this paper when he says, "Reading is something we do, not so much with our eyes, as such, as with our knowledge and interests and enthusiasm, our hatred and fondnesses and fears, our evaluations in all their forms and aspects." The teacher's job is to teach this concept to students and to give them opportunities to give expression to the ideas and feelings that are born as what they have learned in the past combines with the ideas and feelings they experience as they are reading.

Teachers have been concerned about "individualizing" reading instruction ever since the fact of individual differences in learning was accepted by the educational community. Creative reading is a highly individual process. Letting each student supply his personal additions to a particular selection is certainly one dimension of individualizing instruction. Thirty students responding differently to the same story, poem, or newspaper article can be just as much of an individualized reading activity as thirty students responding to thirty different selections. Obviously, students must be taught to learn what the author put on the page before they create additions of their own. But when students have been encouraged to add something to material they have read, teachers must be prepared to accept their creations as expressions of individuality and not expect the work of one student to resemble the work of another student or look like the product the teacher would have created, given the same task.

READING AS THINKING

Creative reading is difficult to define because the nature of the phenomenon is highly individual and complex. Perhaps creative reading can be best conceptualized as a level or kind of thinking behavior. If Bloom's *Taxonomy of Educational Objectives* (1) is used as a reference to specify a particular cognitive level for creative thinking, then the level of "synthesis" seems to provide the best fit. At this level, thinking is the process of working with elements or parts and combining them in such a way as to constitute a pattern or structure not clearly there before. This requires a recombination of parts or all of a previous experience with new material, reconstructed into a new and integrated whole. Applied to reading, this means that ideas acquired from a reading selection are combined with ideas or information acquired elsewhere in a purposeful search for a new product, pattern, or structure (e.g., additional dialogue, an original drawing, a puppet show, a different story ending, a new character).

The images, dialogue, sounds, speculations, and other creations arising in the mind of a reader as spin-offs from an author's words can do much to enhance the understanding and enjoyment of selections that lend themselves to creative thinking. One of the characteristics of reluctant readers, or readers with poorly developed basic reading skills, is that they don't add anything to the material they read. Consequently, they miss the exhilaration that comes from investing something of oneself in a story, poem, or exposition. Otto and Smith (*2*) say, "The student who brings the full range of his thinking and feeling powers to a reading act is a mature reader. He comprehends not only the stated but also the implied meanings of the author ... as he reads, he learns, applies, analyzes, synthesizes, and evaluates. He is satisfied, frustrated, delighted, disquieted."

SPECIAL CHARACTERISTICS OF INTERMEDIATE GRADE CHILDREN

The fostering of creative thinking relative to reading selections is possible and desirable at all academic levels for students who have mastered the basic decoding and comprehension skills. It is during intermediate grades that students appear to have both the maturity and the basic abilities to benefit greatly from well-designed programs.

Torrance (*13*) says, "Children between ten and twelve delight in exploration, girls preferring to explore in books and in pretend play and boys through first-hand experiences. It is a great age for reading. They have now become less restless and can read or think for long periods.... The child at this stage ... is capable of deriving principles or generalizations or devising schemes to express sympathy, if challenged to do so. He seldom does so on his own initiative." Smith and Barrett (*10*) say,

> Although reading may be used to foster creative behavior at all academic levels, the intermediate grades are particularly well suited to this kind of activity. Students in the intermediate grades have a greater wealth of background experiences than primary grade students and are not so inhibited in regard to divergent thinking as older students often become. Both of these characteristics are important to the success of reading-related activities designed to foster creativity. To be creative the student must draw upon his repertoire of experiences and arrange them in a pattern that is different from any previous pattern in his thinking. To do this he must "dare to be different." The playful, yet purposeful, behavior inherent in creativity lends itself well to the mind of the preadolescent.

The emerging importance of the content area curriculums is another factor that causes the intermediate grades to be fertile ground for developing the habit of thinking creatively while reading. After grade three, reading materials in the content areas rapidly become more sophisticated in both the information that is presented and the linguistic structure used to express it. Questions and tasks that encourage students to combine the information they are learning with experiences they have had in other contexts for the creation of some product they can share with interested people can make the reading of content more productive in terms of both enjoyment and information gained.

PROCEDURES THAT ENCOURAGE CREATIVE READING

Undoubtedly, some students learn to respond creatively to reading selections without formal instruction. However, the large number of students at all academic levels who seem unable to respond to a reading selection with more than short answers to factual questions suggests the need for formal instruction in this important dimension of the reading program. Perhaps a major problem is that many reading materials and coordinated instructional activities seem to work against the development of the habit of thinking creatively while reading. Too heavy reliance upon workbooks, kits, and other developmental reading materials in the instructional program may cause students to perceive reading as no more than a matter of superficially reading a short selection (which is often of questionable literary quality) and answering five or ten multiple-choice questions. Many times the questions are constructed to allow students to evaluate their reading ability by checking their answers against an answer key, thereby eliminating any question whose answer requires more than a direct statement or a response of several words. Certainly, these materials give little encouragement to add something to the selection from the students' personal experiences.

Reading Literature

The key to fostering the habit of reading creatively, then, may lie in 1) finding material that has interesting characters and situations, vivid descriptions, well-chosen words, and other features that permit students to empathize, visualize, and think through an idea with an author; and 2) structuring reading-related instructional activities that give students direction and parameters without focusing their thinking so sharply that the process of synthesizing information is stifled or the emergence of personal feelings is repressed.

In *Raccoons Are the Brightest People*, North (6) writes, "Pet deer clearly marked with red ribbons and with antlers stained with Mercurochrome are murdered almost every year by poachers, usually as the trusting animal walks to within ten or fifteen feet of these 'licensed murderers' invading posted land." Teachers might ask students individually, in pairs, or in small groups to use this passage as a point of departure for the following activities:

1. Writing a dialogue between a game warden and a poacher who has just killed a deer illegally.
2. Producing a mock court trial for a man accused of killing an animal out of season.
3. Planning a scene for a movie or a TV drama in which a poacher kills someone's pet. (Lighting, background

music, costumes, close-up shots, setting, and other elements could be taken into consideration.)
4. Writing a letter to the editor from a farmer whose cow was killed by a deer hunter.
5. Creating a lecture that Sterling North might give the members of the National Rifle Association at their annual convention.

These creative activities are good because they are fun to do and because they help students develop their language arts skills. But they also train students to engage in creative thinking while they read. How many readers of Tarzan's adventures have been disappointed in the movie versions because in their creative reading they had imagined his animal friends, his enemies, and his jungle quite differently from the way Hollywood interpreted them? The following passage is taken from *Tarzan and the Lost Safari* (*2*): "At sunrise the next morning Tarzan stirred and rose, stretching, breathing deeply, then bent to add fuel to the small fire, building it up carefully, using wood that burned with little or no smoke." What is Tarzan thinking as he starts the day? What is happening in the jungle around him? How does the start of Tarzan's day compare with the way you start your day?

These are the kinds of questions that get students' imaginations working. The answers are the kinds of thoughts that flit through the minds of creative readers as they process the words and sentences that in one sense are the same for everyone who reads them and in another sense different for everyone who reads them.

Smith (*9*) has prepared guidelines for the construction of questions and tasks designed to stimulate students to think creatively as they read: 1) they ask for information that is not in the material, 2) they ask for the reader's personal ideas, 3) they do not attempt to evoke responses that can be judged as correct or incorrect, and 4) they focus on what the reader can add to the material. Intermediate grade students can learn quickly to recognize questions that send them on a thoughtful, purposeful mental trip beyond the boundaries of the story into unfamiliar territory.

In *The Light in the Forest*, Richter (*8*) writes, "The two marched on in silence. When they came to the river's edge, Half Arrow stepped aside and True Son waded in alone. . . . Not until he was out and dripping on the other side and following the trail on the bank with the column did he look back. Far across the water he could make out two figures. They were Half Arrow and Little Crane, standing at the water's edge. Their eyes he knew strained after him. He wished he could hold up his hand in farewell, but his arms were tied.

Then he passed with his companions into the forest." This is the final paragraph in Chapter Four and a good point of departure for some creative thinking activities. Students at this point in the novel might be asked to do one or more of the following:

1. Imagine Half Arrow and Little Crane returning to their camp. What are their thoughts? What words pass between them? Describe the scene around the Indian campfire that night.
2. If Half Arrow were to make a speech to his tribe that night, what would he say?
3. Write an entry for Little Crane's diary in which he describes the day's events, his feelings, and his speculations about the future.

Writing in the first person, Taylor (*11*) in **The Cay** creates the character of a young man cast away on a lonely Caribbean island with an old black West Indian sailor. Reading about the relationship that grows between the young man and the old sailor—in part because of an injury that blinds the young man—is highly revealing of human nature to many students in the intermediate grades. The story ends with the following passage: "Maybe I won't know it by sight, but when I go ashore and close my eyes, I'll know this was our own cay. I'll walk along east beach and out to the reef. I'll go up the hill to the row of palm trees and stand by his grove." Students enjoy role playing, and this story provides many opportunities for them to create a new character who joins the two castaways at some point in the narrative or for them to plan and present a "Meet the Press" program in which the young man is interviewed by members of the press about his adventures. Or, the young man might play the role of a guest on a late evening talk show of the kind most students in the intermediate grades are familiar with.

Reading in the Content Areas

At some time during the intermediate grades students usually study ecology in their science curriculums. The materials they read might lead to the creation of letters to the editor regarding pollution control, or mock trials of industries accused of polluting rivers with their wastes, or a list of rules for campers to follow—ranging from having their automobiles well tuned to the use of minibikes on forest trails. One science teacher had the animals of the forest sue campers for the anguish and physical damage they had suffered. His seventh graders set up a trial situation with one student representing the deer, another the fish, and others in special roles. The students had to do considerable "noncreative" as well as creative reading for this project.

Language arts teachers might ask students to read a story as a television or movie producer would read it if he were going to adapt it for another medium. Students would be alerted to identify scenes that would be highlighted or cut, settings that would be desirable, actors to play the leading roles, and other aspects that must be considered in television and movie production. Poems often suggest visual images or feelings that can be represented by combinations of colors or abstract drawings. Stanzas can be added to poems and new endings can be supplied for short stories.

Physical education teachers can assign students to read the sports pages in their daily newspapers and write "guess who" dialogues between a quarterback and his coach concerning some performance during the game of the week. Students can be asked to write about the game or one part of the game as a biographer might write about it in "The Story of Johnny Unitas" or "Bobby Hull in Action." Or students can compose a letter that Babe Ruth, if he were alive, might write to Hank Aaron as Aaron broke Ruth's home run record. Or boxing fans can supply the words that might have been exchanged between Joe Frazier and Muhammad Ali in a particular round.

When social studies teachers have ascertained that their students understand what the author of their history text has written about the signing of the Declaration of Independence, the teachers can ask students to engage in one or more of the following activities:

1. You have read that Adams and Franklin made some changes in Jefferson's draft of the Declaration. Pretend that the three of them have met to discuss those changes. Who would begin the conversation? How would Jefferson react to the knowledge that someone had changed what he had written with such emotion and dedication? How might the history of this nation have been changed by the meeting?
2. Imagine that you are a group of colonists in the park reading the Declaration for the first time. How do you feel? What do you say? Do some role playing in small groups.
3. You are a colonist with some artistic talent and you know this Declaration means war and that soldiers will have to be recruited for an army. Design a poster urging able-bodied colonists to enlist in the new colonial army.
4. Write a letter that Benjamin Franklin might have written to a good friend of his in London or in Paris shortly after he signed the Declaration. Remember, he's an old man with much experience and many accomplishments behind him.

GUIDELINES FOR CREATIVE READING INSTRUCTION

The possibilities for training students to let their minds travel some of the side roads as well as the main highways while reading are limited only by the imagination of teachers and their willingness to construct questions and activities that introduce students to the many possibilities for divergent thinking that present themselves in reading selections. Teachers should be aware of certain conditions that must be present if the objectives of creative reading are to be attained:

1. The material must be suitable for creative thinking. Tasks that are strained to fit unsuitable material usually result in strained or illogical responses.
2. Students need time for the synthesizing process to work. Creativity cannot be rushed.
3. Students and teachers must learn that products resulting from creative thinking relative to reading selections cannot be graded or evaluated as correct or incorrect.
4. The questions and tasks that are assigned must be reasonable expectations of the students who receive them. Few, if any, students in the intermediate grades can redesign a skyscraper or write an original musical score for *Tarzan and the Jewels of Opar*.

SUMMARY

A reading selection, a carefully constructed task to stimulate creative thinking about that selection, and the mind of a student in the intermediate grades can become a powerful combination for generating an original idea or product. Important also to the process of creation is an environment that encourages a searching mind and provides time to let that mind synthesize information and feelings arising from a variety of experiences. Teachers must provide all of the conditions that foster creativity if students are to learn to use reading as a springboard to a new idea, feeling, or tangible product.

Learning to think creatively while one reads is like most other learned behaviors. Students need instruction, practice, and positive reinforcement for their efforts. They especially need teachers who believe that the fostering of creative thinking relative to a reading selection is an important objective of the reading curriculum.

References

1. Bloom, Benjamin et al. *Taxonomy of Educational Objectives*. New York: McKay, 1956.
2. Burroughs, Edgar Rice. *Tarzan and the Lost Safari*. Racine, Wisconsin: Whitman Publishing, 1966, 122.
3. Frick, C. H. *The Comeback Guy*. New York: Harcourt, Brace and World, 1961, 76.
4. Gibran, Kahlil. "On Teaching," *The Prophet*. New York: Alfred A. Knopf, 1965, 56.
5. Johnson, Wendell. *Your Most Enchanted Listener*. New York: Harper and Row, 1956, 123.
6. North, Sterling. *Raccoons Are the Brightest People*. New York: Avon Books, 1966, 157.
7. Otto, Wayne, and Richard J. Smith. *Administering the School Reading Program*. Boston: Houghton Mifflin, 1970, 72.
8. Richter, Conrad. *The Light in the Forest*. New York: Bantam Books, 1953, 22.
9. Smith, Richard J. "Questions for Teachers—Creative Reading," *Reading Teacher*, February 1969, 430-434, 439.
10. Smith, Richard J., and Thomas C. Barrett. *Teaching Reading in the Middle Grades*. Reading, Massachusetts: Addison-Wesley, 1974.
11. Taylor, Theodore. *The Cay*. New York: Avon Books, 1969, 144.
12. Torrance, E. P. "Guidelines for Creative Teaching," *High School Journal*, 1965, 459-464.
13. Torrance, E. Paul. *Guiding Creative Talent*. Englewood Cliffs, New Jersey: Prentice-Hall, 1964, 97.

CREATIVITY IN SECONDARY SCHOOLS

Jo Brazell
Carmel, California, Unified School District

The age of the moon shot, technical know-how, and the computer is also the age of educational frustration—frustration on the part of the educator who would like to have the time and the opportunity to teach; frustration on the part of those students who would like to become more involved in the educational process; and frustration on the part of those who find the educational process too difficult, too overwhelming, and, too often, nonmotivating.

CONTEMPORARY PROBLEMS

Schools are crowded and demands are increasing, just as funds seem to be decreasing. The teacher sometimes finds himself involved in schizophrenic role playing—taking the place of the parent, the minister, the doctor, and the counselor, with little time left for his professional role as the educator.

Today's educator of emerging adolescents is also being placed in an awkward situation. In a relatively new role, the educator is expected to provide training in skills that will enable these students to hold jobs and to use materials that have not yet been developed. Thus it becomes the duty of the educator to provide the student with twofold skills: those needed to make a living and those needed to live an enriched life.

Because of pressures brought on by increasing amounts of subject matter and by an overflowing quantity of terminology, educators find themselves resorting to irrelevant and superficial questions that require "exact" answers: questions that deal with unimportant pieces of information; questions that encourage guessing without bothering to probe the statement; and questions that are often ambiguous in structure. A structure of this type seems to permit more to be covered in a shorter period of time and to be easier to evaluate. In order to relieve further pressures, a do-it-yourself movement of programed and computerized packages seems to be infiltrating the market.

DEMANDS FOR RELEVANCE

The demands made upon the average adolescent student have steadily increased. The competition for college entrance and suitable jobs has become so intense that educators are beginning to see the need for completely reorganizing the educational structure. Education has become such a vast transcript of written material that even the most academic and talented student cannot begin to make a dent in it. What is relevant in the spectrum of skills today may be only unimportant historical facts in a few years. Because of these pressures, it has become increasingly important to train students to become both functional and creative readers.

Since today's student finds himself living in a critical period, classroom skills must become more than a veneer to education. They must become functional by helping the student to develop the ability to be a critical reader, to correlate and integrate information, to read between and beyond the lines, and to utilize to the fullest extent the cognitive and affective domain.

A teacher needs all the help possible to really teach each student to read the lines, read between the lines, read beyond the lines, and develop these necessary skills. Too often, one feels that team teaching, teaching aides, self-teaching machines, and materials will provide the individualized instruction that appears to be necessary for all children to succeed. Unfortunately, educators often overlook a resource group that needs specialized help—creative students.

CREATIVE EVOLUTION

Although creativity is the oldest recorded educational concept (the book of Genesis), the study of what constitutes creative thinking is still a pioneer venture. Too often, under the guise of creative dramatics or creative writing, the student is still faced with limitations of previous styles and with basic English rules imposed by the teacher.

Man, however, is not just a cognitive being. He is sensitive to the existence of certain stimuli and reacts favorably or negatively towards them. Imagery, as well as emotion, is an important factor in the ability to grasp meaning. As he encounters various situations, man begins to internalize values and to integrate his attitudes into his total philosophy. Educators are becoming more aware of the fact that the senses are never fully developed to their capacity. To become more articulate, one learns many ways to say the same thing.

In dealing with the basic tool of the educational system—the book—the questions that an educator should ask himself are:

1. How can a student become flexible enough to make his

reading skills function for him outside of the literature class?
2. How can a student be freed from being tied to the literal word as he translates the author's message?
3. How can the student best be trained to detect the implied meanings presented by the author?
4. How can the student efficiently reorganize what he reads into newly correlated and integrated concepts?
5. How can a student let his imagination soar beyond the printed word in order to create new ideas never before expressed?
6. How can these reorganized and imagined ideas be produced in concrete creations without the fear of exposing one's self to ridicule as others experience the end product?
7. How can one train students to use cognitive maps as they make sensory searches?

Psychologists and medical doctors speak of the "whole" person and his experiences. If this is the case, students must be immersed totally in the educational process; must become aware that their education may come to them via different routes—visually, aurally, orally, kinesthetically; and must be motivated to learn and encouraged to share their knowledge.

Since the utilization of reading skills enables each student to cultivate his own talents and to develop self-realization, human relationships, economic efficiency, and civic responsibility, a functional and meaningful goal in the educational process is achieved by the educator who teaches these skills. Training one to use his skills, to transfer skills to other areas, to see the purpose of reading, and to develop self-motivation no longer limits education to a self-realization that occurs in the basic reading program from grades one to six. Instead, education becomes a lifelong adventure of skill building, application, reorganization, and creation.

To accomplish the training which will enable a student to become a functional, critical, and creative reader, teaching strategies must change. Teachers must utilize material that will enable the student to develop the ability to receive ideas, utilize them, test them, and throw them into fresh combinations. In other words, the teacher must help students develop the ability to interpolate, extrapolate, and project.

INHIBITORS TO CREATIVITY

Unfortunately, research in the area of creativity has focused on understanding the nature of creativity and the creative person, rather than on developing materials. There are inhibitors that affect the growth of creativity in the classroom. Education has become specialized. Students see subject matter as something segmented; they do not see its relationships. Most of the educational texts are based on the lower realms of the cognitive domain that encourage convergent rather than divergent thinking. There is also a misconception that the "3 Rs" might be discarded in a creative curriculum rather than used as tools in developing higher skills.

Too often, by the end of the first or second grade, educators have instilled in the student the fear that he is running a risk when he makes mistakes. The student soon becomes reluctant to take a chance and begins to cling to accepted patterns. In order to get along, the student must surrender himself to be constantly screened, classified, tested, scheduled, programed, and conditioned by the school. This form of desensitization alienates the student from his work and produces a nonmotivated student who either conforms or is such a threat to the educator that he often becomes a discipline problem. During his twelve years in school, this student may become sterotyped, stamped, sealed, and delivered to society to play the role expected of him—that of a conformist. Or, as is currently apparent, he may assume the role of a nonconformist without any guidelines at all.

CREATIVE REALITIES

How can educators, then, make creativity a reality in which the inner words not audible to the ear but audible to the listening mind and heart can be brought forth to be shared and valued rather than remaining unexpressed, displaced, repressed, and finally obliterated?

Telling a student to read or write creatively is obviously futile. The student learns at an early age not to take risks, and in creative reading and writing classes he may safeguard his security by expressing himself in some incident which will be accepted by the teacher because it conforms to an approved topic, manner of expression, vocabulary, and length. Creative reading and writing must become much more than this form of approved recall. Time spans of remembrance, intimate emotional responses, complete grasp of imagery—all must be reflected in the character of the work as the student reads and writes.

How does one go about developing a creative learning atmosphere? Readiness for germinating creativity could stem from the hierarchical arrangement of the critical thinking process. The classroom educator seldom utilizes taxonomy. Materials could be developed that would enable the student to go beyond commonplace education that seems to encompass only knowledge and comprehension. Hopefully, through the use of taxonomy, which would require students to look at the same material in many different ways, the student could be brought to maturity as a reader. These questions could deal with 1) basic cognitive goals—knowledge, comprehension, application, analysis, synthesis, and evaluation—and 2) the affective goals—receiving, responding, valuing, organizing values, and achieving a way of behaving which is characterized by a value system.

Two new areas have recently appeared on the educational frontier as attempts to induce creative thinking:

1. *Synectics* (The study of creative processes; the solution of problems in diverse ways.) This educational concept stresses spontaneous expression of ideas that are free from critical judgment.

2. *Morphological analysis* (The study of the meaning bearing units of the language and of how these units function; the formation of new words from internal elements of our language; the development of a communication framework.) This educational concept considers all possible combinations—even the coining of new words.

Although researchers may use different terminology, they agree that the most common characteristics found in the creative process are fluency, flexibility, originality, and elaboration. Materials could be produced that would develop the student's ability to: write or draw in quantitative measures, adjust and adapt anything, rearrange and regroup words that are read, go beyond what has been written, create something novel, and add the needed unique details.

IMAGERY EXPANSION

One would think the head would ache from carrying around accumulating files of knowledge, audiovisual materials, and sensory aids. Although this is an absurd comparison, it is exactly what imagery does. Mental pictures or symbols are classified, stored, and recalled when the need arises or when some stimulus evokes a response. Imagination enables one to expand rather than to contract his creative abilities. Imagery is so valuable and so economical—it is unhampered by lack of resources—that it should be investigated.

There are basically four kinds of creative imagery for which materials could be developed:

1. The ability to imagine one's self as the object or the subject.
2. The ability to study a process in order to create something new.
3. The ability to compare things symbolic through the use of metaphors and similies.

4. The ability to free the imagination from its normal boundaries in the form of fantasy.

Other creative language activities could include: developing open-ended sentences and stories; using day and night dreams as sources of language experience stories; recognizing a problem, analyzing it, suggesting possible solutions or consequences, testing it, and judging one's results; triggering responses that could arouse more than one sensory image simultaneously; and finally, playing with words and their meanings by rearranging, transforming, expanding, and reducing sentences.

Since historical situations condition creativity, since creative potential emerges when a student becomes totally immersed in a problem, since recurring themes can be placed in different contexts—thus dissolving already formed boundaries—since the arts can be used to reflect man's feeling generated by his environment, and since the arts are creative acts of symbolic languages, the humanities—now more than ever before—have a vital place in the creative curriculum.

MINIEDUCATORS

Education must be meaningful to the student. He must feel included in curriculum planning and totally involved in the general educational process. The ability of the creative student to develop innovative materials, to correlate and integrate curriculum, and to explain problems in a unique manner must be capitalized upon. The development of classroom miniteachers rather than classroom aides utilizes the potential powerhouse of creative energy found in every class and to some degree in every student.

Why would one train these students to become "miniteachers"? The reasons will become clear after reviewing some of the general strategies available to the teacher.

As the teacher applies his energies to the educational task, he often turns to technology as an aid in individualizing instruction. The amount of hardware and software found on the market is overwhelming and the cost is high. Technology offers the teacher, who can't work with each child at the same time, a form of patient repetition. This repetition is offered in numerous packages of skills called "computerized learning." Another aid is found in the program that offers minute, detailed explanations with a built-in opportunity to immediately check one's answers. This is known as "programed learning."

Tape recorders make it possible to record one's oral discourse and play it back. Reading pacers and other speed machines can force the reader to move along as he reads. Although all of these machines and the supplementary material that accompany these programs have assets, something is still lacking. Since "no man is an island," the student needs to communicate. He needs meaningful dialogue which gives him the chance to test his answers, seek solutions to problems, evaluate and weigh what is being said, learn through meaningful discussion, and ask the proverbial question "why?"

As one learns, he is like an athlete, drilling and repeating exercises until the skill becomes purposeful and almost automatic. Each new skill prepares him for another step up the learning ladder. But the athlete cannot work up to par excellence by himself; he needs a coach to check his every move, offer suggestions, and encourage him whether he fails or succeeds, and so does the learner. Unfortunately, the teacher finds himself unable to give the desired personalized attention at the time the student needs it the most. The school cannot supply a teacher for each child, nor would it be practical to do so.

This need, however, could be filled by a miniteacher who has experienced the same problems but, for some reason, has not experienced the same frustrations. This void could be filled by someone who has empathy with another student in a similar learning situation.

These students seem to have the uncanny gift of explaining in their own language what teachers are unable to do when teaching a group. Often, however, when these students are called upon to help as tutors, the teacher stifles their creative abilities by imposing his own methods upon them.

The student tutor has other assets. He not only speaks the same language but also, because there is no generation gap, is able to face the problem on an even keel with the student he is helping. Sometimes the educator unconsciously lets his bias and experience get in his way and either overwhelms the student with his multiapproach methods or confuses him with his oversimplified explanation.

One tends to shortchange these tutors, however, by denying them the opportunity of understanding some of the basic philosophy of education and the rationale for using certain materials and methods. Operating in the dark would make the work of these tutors less effective than it could be.

How does one train these students to become miniteachers with a sound educational background and yet allow them to explore academically, creatively, and individually the possibilities of teaching reading or any other subject in an innovative manner? In order to do this successfully, a sound methodology course must be offered to them by means of continuous inservice workshops. These workshops can be offered by district or county specialists, publishing companies, and local resource people.

When one tutors, he is not a fill-in teacher, nor does he use a hit-or-miss procedure. His program, under the guidance of the teaching staff, must be structured and constantly reorganized and evaluated. He must know what is to be expected of his pupil, know when the educational objectives have been achieved, know what experiences are necessary to achieve the objectives, know the pupil for whom he is designing the experience, and know how to evaluate the degree of change in behavior.

This means that the tutors work closely with the teacher. Developing this program is a slow process, but although it takes time, the program is worthwhile and necessary. This is the reason why the secondary student must become the key factor in this creative educational evolution. He has many of the traditional basic facts under his belt; he is still receptive to changes; he is a dynamo of energy and can put new innovations into practice. This age group has ample time to develop talents throughout the secondary school years and the chance to establish a workable program. It also might be noted that one can be developing very critical clients for the future teaching profession.

The teaching staff and resource people can help in further training of these tutors by offering workshops in some of the following areas:

1. Art department—making and packaging individualized learning material into an attractive format.
2. Secretarial staff—instructing tutors on how to use some of the various machines for reproducing and organizing material; advising students how to use their time economically in order to work at a higher efficiency rate.
3. Physical Education department—developing a kinesthetic approach to learning.
4. Music department—preparing visual tracking exercises and auditory approaches to learning.
5. Math department—applying readability formulas to textbooks in order to aid teachers and students in understanding the level of reading difficulty. This is valuable in understanding the independent level, instructional level, and the frustration level in reading; and it is also valuable in knowing how to pace a student.
6. Publishers—presenting the philosophy of the program and demonstrating the special approaches necessary in order to get the maximum response from the students.

7. English and Social Studies departments—developing in the student an awareness that written and spoken language varies in structure depending upon the situation.
8. Foreign Language department—instructing tutors how to use the listening lab with their students in order to get practice in oral reading, in replay of tape with critical analysis, and in listening to imitate proper phrasing and expression. These tapes would also be of great value to the tutor and the teacher as they further plan individualized instruction for the student. To facilitate diagnosis of specific skills that need to be developed, it is suggested that the tutor be instructed on how to record in consistent form the mistakes made by the pupil as he reads orally.

Each of the above groups of resource people can also be helpful in developing skills and technical vocabulary specific to each content area; in developing methods of reading each subject's symbolic language; and in creating innovative games, drill material, and tests.

SUMMARY

If one is to utilize creativity in an effort to make curriculum and educational changes, one must attempt to meet the following educational challenges:

1. To immerse the student totally in time-space creative activities, a cross-fertilization of ancient ideas with modern concepts may prove to be necessary.
2. To develop the primary source of creativity, imagery and ideational flows, methods must be developed that do not rely solely on talent, socioeconomic conditions, and motor skills.
3. To develop functional reading skills, previous skills must be regrouped, reorganized, and used in new situations.
4. To develop a readiness for creativity, a hierarchy of critical thinking/reading skills must be established.
5. To develop the complete spectrum of creative imagery, one's personal analogy, direct analogy, symbolic analogy, and fantasy must be developed.
6. To develop motivation, attitudes must be changed.
7. To make education a cooperative lifelong adventure, giving of one's self to help his fellow student makes learning a rewarding educational process.

PART THREE

MATERIALS AND RESOURCES

The task of *fostering reading growth* requires special materials and resources at the primary, intermediate, and secondary levels. While maintaining a thread of similarity, each chapter in this section indicates that unique differences do exist at each level. However, education should be seen primarily as a totality of experiences. Thus, to assume that a certain content belongs permanently at one grade level and not at another would be contrary to the concept of individualization.

As principals and teachers adapt their programs to foster creative reading for the gifted, they will find helpful the stimulating ideas of specific materials and resources suggested for various grade levels. Recommendations for a creative atmosphere and a variety of materials to be made by teachers, pupils, and others should trigger countless ideas for adapting available materials to the differences in pupils' reading levels, skills, and interests. Requirements for bona fide creativity training activities and appropriate teaching strategies will suggest to teachers many ideas for specific activities suitable for their programs.

M.L.

FOSTERING READING GROWTH FOR GIFTED AND CREATIVE READERS AT THE PRIMARY LEVEL

Carl J. Wallen
Arizona State University

The most difficult and demanding task facing the primary grade teacher is also the most important—adjusting instruction to the individual differences of children. These differences range all the way from James, who comes to the first grade able to read the newspaper, to Pete, who cannot yet even recognize his own name. Contrary to popular practice, the adjustment is not best accomplished by using one set of methods and materials with children whose IQ is below 125 and another with those having IQs above 125. Some would suggest (*10*) that nongifted children should be given a basal reader method while gifted are given an individualized method. In commenting on programs suggested for the gifted, Tinker and McCullough (*11*) noted that the activities described represent "good procedure for all children...." Bond and Wagner (*2*) pointed out that

> The adjustment of instruction to individual differences is more than a method. It is an attitude—an attitude in which the teacher assumes that each child has a right to progress as rapidly as he is capable, that each child can expect the school to provide for his rate of learning, be it slow or fast, and that each child can expect the school to study him as an individual and to help him when he is in difficulty.

The approach of using special methods and materials with special groups of children is related to the grade-conscious orientation that Austin and Morrison (*1*) identified in their classical study of the teaching of reading. They concluded that

> Too many elementary school teachers apparently have been unable to discard the concept that they are third or fourth grade teachers. Consequently, they feel compelled to teach the subject matter and skills which they consider suitable for their grade irrespective of differences that may exist among children. These teachers expect all the children in their classes to read from the same page of the same book.

The current emphasis on special methods and materials usually results in poor education for the gifted because, in the opinion of Smith and Dechant (*9*), it is "... extremely difficult to help the gifted achieve maximum growth under a system that must frequently be geared to the needs of the average or even the dull child."

It seems to this writer that the approach of relating methods and materials to special groups of children is in turn a symptom of a greater problem, materialism. Characteristically, we look to producers of material things to solve our nonmaterial problems. We look to Detroit to solve the very transportation problems they were instrumental in creating. The fact that we devote forty percent of our cities to the automobile will probably not be changed by making automobile engines that produce less pollution. If we want to do something about transportation, we must look at the basic process itself and ask about the goals of transportation and our needs relative to those goals. The result of that examination may well be something as radical as banning the automobile.

In considering the topic of reading and the gifted, we might avoid the usual consequences of our materialism if we begin with the basic goals of reading and then examine needs relative to those goals. We should avoid the rather natural materialistic tendency to ask, "What are the methods and materials that should be provided gifted children?"

READING GOALS

The basic goals of reading lie in two areas—cognitive and affective. In the cognitive area, we hope children will become skillful readers; in the affective area, we hope they will use reading as a means of accomplishing ends that are important to them. Gifted children have special needs relative to the objectives of reading. Their cognitive development is so advanced that the materials and activities normally provided for children at their age and grade levels are so easy for them that they benefit little from instruction. Too, their affective development is generally such that they do not have to be motivated to read, in the traditional sense. All they usually need is time and a purpose.

Cognitive and affective goals are suggested. The goals are appropriate for all readers, not just those classified as gifted.

Cognitive Goals

The cognitive goals that have been identified as being appropriate for gifted readers vary from the suggestion of Gowan and Scheibel (*4*) that the only goal need be "increasing the reading rate," to suggestions that identify lists of objectives much like those considered appropriate for any comprehensive reading program (*3, 6*). The common element of the suggestions is a realization that gifted readers in the primary grades have usually mastered recognition skills—they are able to pronounce most words in a fourth or fifth level reading text—and so will benefit most from instruction for comprehension skills.

A suggested list of comprehension skills is drawn from two sources (*12, 8*). The abilities referred to in each are described in parentheses.

WORD MEANING
(Able to define and/or exemplify the meaning of specified words.)

PARAGRAPH MEANING
Recall
1. Recall-Identification
   (Able to recall specific items that were directly mentioned in the selection. The selection may be as short as a word or as long as a number of sentences.)
2. Recall-Organization
   (Able to organize specific items differently from the way they were presented in the story. The organization should reflect the relationship between specific items.)

Interpretation
1. Interpretation-Summarization
   (Able to identify the major idea presented in the entire selection or in a designated section of it.)
2. Interpretation-Conclusion
   (Able to identify underlying ideas in an unstated cause-effect relationship that can be logically inferred from directly stated items in the selection.)

Extrapolation
1. Extrapolation-Consequence
   (Able to use a previously identified cause-effect relationship to infer the consequences of changing either the cause or effect item.)
2. Extrapolation-Analogy
   (Able to use a previously identified cause-effect relationship to infer what an analogous one might be.)

Evaluation
1. Evaluation-Objective
   (Able to make judgements about the reasonableness or soundness of statements or events in a selection based on an internal criterion, such as supporting evidence, reasons, or logic provided in the selection.)

2. Evaluation-Subjective
> (Able to make judgements about statements or events in the selection based on a criterion external to it, such as his own biases, beliefs, or preferences.

RATE
> (Able to vary reading rate according to purposes for reading and the requirements of the selection.)

STUDY SKILLS

Location Skills
> (Able to use pagination, alphabetization, indexes, tables of contents, and other organizing principles in efficiently finding information stored in telephone books, dictionaries, cookbooks, encyclopedias, fiction and nonfiction books, microfilm, card catalogues, and computers.)

Organization Skills
> (Able to use outlining, summarizing, and note taking to put information that has been obtained in some useful order.)

Affective Goals

Gifted children may come to regard school with indifference or with positive distaste because they find nothing interesting to do there (5). A list of affective goals that might be appropriate is suggested.

SHARING
> (Utilizing special talents in individual assignments that are shared in some manner with the class.)

PLANNING AND ORGANIZING READING EFFORTS
> (Developing discrimination, purpose for reading, and criteria for selecting books that can be read and enjoyed.)

PURSUIT OF INTERESTS
> (Having the time to simply enjoy doing things of interest.)

Considerations of goals for reading might be guided by what Sebesta and Wallen (7) suggest are the basic purposes for having reading instruction.

> He who reads is able to negotiate his world with firmer understanding— to control some of the strands of his destiny: the long step from ignorance to wisdom. And he who reads is enabled to find surcease from the pressures inherent in our patterns of living. They are the age-old purposes given new hope: the purposes of knowledge and sanctuary.

SELECTION OF SUITABLE INSTRUCTIONAL MATERIALS

Growth requires challenge; this is the idea behind the developmental sequence built into most instructional materials in reading.

To guide a child in developing his reading skills, we provide books that are sufficiently difficult to be challenging. Matching book difficulty to a child's identified level of skill development has been defined as *instructional level*; i.e., he is able to pronounce correctly 93-98 percent of the words and is able to answer adequately 75-90 percent of the questions he is asked. This particular match of book difficulty and a child's skill is intended to provide an optimal setting for instruction because it encourages the child to grow in his use of reading skills.

Unfortunately, too few children are provided an appropriate challenge because their teachers take their cues from the labels on texts rather than from the children's individual skill development. The teachers too often mistakenly assume that the number four on a basal text means fourth grade, and they assign texts accordingly. The tendency to read labels rather than children is illustrated in a study of the basal text assignment of children conducted by the writer in 1970. In school district A, the children were reading *above* the national average. In school district B, the children were reading *below* the national average. The teachers in both school districts provided the standardized reading achievement scores and basal text assignments of each child in their classroom. It was assumed that a child was reading at a suitable instructional level if his basal text assignment was no more than one year above or below his score on the standardized reading achievement tests. Thus, if a child's reading achievement score was 3.5, he would be considered to be placed at his instructional level if he were assigned to a basal text having a level of 3, 4, or 5; placement in a sixth level book would be considered at a frustration level; and placement in a second level book would be considered at an independent level. Even with this wide range of instructional levels, it was found that about one-third of the children in district A (reading above national norms) were assigned books which were at the independent level, with almost no children assigned books which were at the frustration level. In district B (reading below national norms) the situation was just the reverse: about one-third of the children were assigned books which were at the frustration level, and almost none were given books at the independent level. The same phenomenon would appear to be operating in both school districts: the teachers tended to assign children on the basis of grade level rather than achievement level.

The conclusion seems rather clear. If teachers are to provide instructional materials that encourage growth, then they must be ready to provide a variety of books at a child's instructional level. Many of the better readers, those we might call gifted, will require books two or more levels above their grade level. Some second grade children should be given sixth level books, and some sixth grade children should be given college texts. The teacher can better challenge the gifted reader to grow a bit by basing text assignments upon achievement level rather than upon grade level. In addition to providing materials at different reading levels, the teacher should also make readily available a wide variety of printed materials, such as books encompassing various topics, children's encyclopedias, dictionaries, magazines, and weekly papers.

But reading should not be confused with printed materials. All sorts of other-than-book media should be used to carry other-than-print messages. Audiovisual devices can play an important role in providing experiences for the child.

TEACHING FOR COGNITIVE GOALS

After providing the child with materials that are at an appropriate level of difficulty, the next task is to identify instructional exercises that are suitable for each child's specific skill needs. Teachers are seriously mistaken when they assume that a child's specific skill needs are directly indicated by a general reading achievement score; the score is only an average of subtest scores. The very process of averaging often hides the actual variation in subtest scores. For example, John's reading achievement score is 6.8; on the subtest for paragraph meaning he received 5.8 and for word meaning 7.8 which averages out to 6.8. Mary's reading achievement score is 4.3; her paragraph meaning score is 3.6 and her word meaning score is 4.9. The teacher should realize that even the subtest scores for paragraph meaning and word meaning are in themselves derived by averaging specific items. John's paragraph meaning score of 5.8 probably hides a wide variation in his attainment of the specific skills that constitute the large category called paragraph meaning.

When the teacher fails to identify the most appropriate instructional exercises for a child, and simply gives him the exercises other children are receiving with the justification that a little review never hurt anyone, the teacher is committing an error that is commonly made with gifted children. Even a little review may hurt the child since a child is always hurt when he is not learning. He is hurt because he is not gaining new skills, which he can use just as much as any other child; and he is hurt because a rehashing of old material is uninteresting. What the gifted child needs is what all children need—instruction that is appropriate for his particular needs. A good way to provide instruction appropriate for specific reading skills needs is to utilize a criterion-referenced approach.

Criterion-Referenced Approach

Criterion-referencing is relating the activities of testing and teaching to specific skill objectives. It is accomplished by designing a test and a lesson for each specific objective. For example, there would be a separate test and lesson for each of these specific objectives.

1. Recall-organization: literature, fifth level.
2. Evaluation-objective: science, third level.
3. Rate: social science, fourth level.
4. Extrapolation-analogy: literature, sixth level.

The test for each specific skill objective is administered to a child; he then receives the lesson for the objective only if he performs inadequately on the test for the objective. In this way the teacher provides a child with only those specific lessons that are appropriate for him.

With a criterion-referenced system, the teacher orients instruction to the child's learning rather to her own teaching. Because many teachers are oriented to their own teaching, they have a difficult time accepting the fact that a child could attain an objective like *Evaluation-objective: science, third level* without ever having been taught it. Gifted children learn many things without formal teaching. Since the capacity for independent learning is, after all, what makes them gifted. The teacher's challenge is to identify reading skill objectives a child has not already attained independently.

There are a number of criterion-referenced reading systems presently on the market, and one or two more appear each year. But teachers need not depend upon publishers to produce criterion-referenced systems; they can develop their own. Many teachers have developed very effective criterion-referenced reading systems by cooperatively following a procedure of 1) identifying a suitable list of reading skill objectives, 2) assigning teachers to design tests for certain objectives, 3) assigning teachers to design lessons and identify suitable instructional materials for certain objectives, and 4) producing tests and lessons in sufficient quantity for each participating teacher to have a complete set. The major advantage of teachers developing their own criterion-referenced system is that they will be the master of the system they develop. Teachers familiar with commercially produced criterion-referenced systems are well aware that they are usually so complex that the teacher has a difficult time remaining the master of the reading program. Havelock Ellis once noted that the greatest task for civilization is to make man rather than machines the master.

A criterion-referenced approach can be used with any method—individualized reading, basal readers, language experience, programed, or whatever may be invented next year. A criterion-referenced approach is used when four steps are followed (*13*).

1. Identify a specific performance objective.
2. Test the children to identify those who have not already attained the objective. A child needs instruction for the objective if he performs inadequately on a test designed for the objective.
3. Teach those children who showed that they need instruction for the objective.
4. Retest to make certain that the children have attained the objective and if some have not, provide additional instruction.

The four-step procedure can be used with any method or set of materials the teacher happens to be using, whether commercially published or teacher made.

When teachers use a criterion-referenced approach in teaching reading skills they have a very clear idea of what each child is learning; and if they maintain records of children's attainment of those objectives, they can demonstrate that learning to principals, fellow teachers, parents, and to themselves.

TEACHING FOR AFFECTIVE GOALS

Cognitive goals differ from affective goals in that the former generally refer to products while the latter refer to processes.

Cognitive goals can usually be operationalized into performances that are testable: reading achievement tests provide global measures of children's attainment of cognitive goals and a criterion-referenced approach depends upon an operational relationship between objectives and children's performance. But affective goals can seldom be operationalized into identified performances; to do so usually invalidates the goal. How, for example, does a creatively written story differ from one that is not? Creativity is a process and as such is not easily reducible to products.

In organizing instructional experiences appropriate for affective goals, the emphasis should be on the process of children doing activities rather than on what they produce in an activity. For example, children might be encouraged to visit the library and select books that interest them and then be given time during the school day to read these books. If the teacher really wants children to **read for enjoyment** (a process) she will not introduce a product measure such as a visual display of the number of books each child has read: "Read twenty books and reach the moon."

Teachers often face a conflict in organizing learning centers when they must decide whether the centers should be for affective or cognitive goals. Does the teacher want the child to learn *something* or does she want him to simply be *involved* in the process of learning? Does she want the child to read twenty books or does she want him to read for enjoyment? Seldom are the two objectives compatible. A child reading for enjoyment may select a book so large that by the time the contest is over he will have only traveled one book length. The child interested in getting to the moon will select short books that can be skimmed quickly and then claimed as accomplishments.

One advantage of using a criterion-referenced approach for cognitive goals is that it provides concrete information about children's learning, so the teacher is usually more willing to let children spend time in process activities that do not result in products that can be graded and taken home. And the parent who has seen records of the specific reading skill objectives his child has attained is more willing to tolerate the fact that his child seems to spend a lot of time "just fooling around" at school.

SUMMARY

Adjusting instruction to the individual needs of children is a difficult and demanding task for the teacher. It is particularly difficult with gifted children because the materials and methods developed for average children are inappropriate for the gifted. But the solution does not lie in identifying the materials and methods suitable for gifted children. Rather, it is best accomplished by utilizing a criterion-referenced approach in achieving cognitive goals and in emphasizing process in achieving affective goals.

References

1. Austin, Mary C., and Coleman Morrison. *The First R: The Harvard Report of Reading in Elementary School.* New York: Macmillan, 1963, 81.
2. Bond, Guy L., and Eva Bond Wagner. *Teaching the Child to Read* (rev. ed.). New York: Macmillan, 1950, 61.
3. DeBoer, John J. "Creative Reading and the Gifted Student," *Reading Teacher*, 16 (May 1963), 435-441.
4. Gowan, J. C., and R. W. Scheibel. "The Improvement of Reading in Gifted Children," *Educational Administration and Supervision*, 46 (January 1960), 35-40.
5. Hollingworth, Leta S. *Children above 180 IQ.* Yonkers, New York: World Book, 1942.

6. Murphy, Geraldine J. "The Education of Gifted Children: Suggestions for a Philosophy and a Curriculum," *School Review*, 62 (October 1954), 414-419.
7. Sebesta, Sam L., and Carl J. Wallen. *The First R: Readings on Teaching Reading*. Chicago: Science Research Associates, 1972.
8. Seymour, John, and Carl J. Wallen. *Paragraph Meaning: Study Skills*. Albany, Oregon: Albany Printing, 1973, 2.
9. Smith, Henry P., and Emerald V. Dechant. *Psychology in Teaching Reading*. Englewood Cliffs, New Jersey: Prentice-Hall, 1961, 392.
10. Spache, George D., and Evelyn B. Spache. *Reading in the Elementary School* (3rd ed.). Boston: Allyn and Bacon, 1973, 326.
11. Tinker, Miles A., and Constance M. McCullough. *Teaching Elementary Reading* (3rd ed.). New York: Appleton-Century-Crofts, 1968, 110.
12. Wallen, Carl J. *Competency in Teaching Reading*. Chicago: Science Research Associates, 1972.
13. Wallen, Carl J. "Independent Activities: A Necessity, Not a Frill," *Reading Teacher*, 27 (December 1973), 257-262.

FOSTERING CREATIVE READING AT THE INTERMEDIATE LEVEL

Robert E. Shafer
Arizona State University

MATURATION TASKS

In his newly revised *Developmental Tasks in Education*, Havighurst (4) proposes that there is a period of life called "middle childhood" which ranges from about 6 to 12 years of age and is characterized by three great outward pushes: 1) the thrust of the child out of the home and into the peer group; 2) the physical thrust into the world of games and work which requires the development of neuromuscular skills; and 3) the mental thrust into the world of adult concepts, logic, symbolism, and communication. Havighurst further proposes that by the end of middle childhood the individual has worked out his particular style and his level in all three areas. Havighurst pictures the beginning of this period as a period of great potential where, within the child, there are untold resources waiting to be realized through the unfolding powers of his body and mind and through the learning experiences he will have in the interaction with his society. Havighurst proposes that the tasks are as follows:
1. Learning physical skills necessary for ordinary games.
2. Building wholesome attitudes toward one's self as a growing organism.
3. Learning to get along with age mates.
4. Learning an appropriate masculine or feminine role.
5. Developing fundamental skills in reading, writing, and calculating.
6. Developing concepts necessary for everyday living.
7. Developing conscience, morality, and a scale of values.
8. Achieving personal independence.
9. Developing attitudes towards social groups and institutions.

Independence and Creative Reading Skills

Almost all of the developmental tasks listed by Havighurst are to a considerable extent related to reading instruction in the intermediate years. Space does not permit the exploration of the many varieties of implications stemming from current research in human development which ultimately will affect reading instruction. We might more profitably consider the implications of this research for the development of specific skills necessary for independent and creative reading of gifted young people attempting to achieve these developmental tasks in the middle years. How can reading help them?

We might look briefly at the middle childhood within the total area of human development as we consider the role reading is to play in it. Piaget has noted that with respect to the development of thought in the child—from the stage of egocentric and rather inaccurate thinking at the age of the beginning of school through the age of "concrete operations" in middle childhood and on to the beginning stage of "formal intellectual operations" from 12 to 14 years—the child passes through various phases of interaction with his environment, including school. All of this interaction facilitates his development through a particular stage. Piaget (*11*) further notes a logical development of thinking based on the experience provided by the same physical and social environment which can be affected by skillful teaching.

Developing Concepts

With respect to the development of intellect, by the time a child is ready for school he already has several hundred concepts—mainly the simple ones learned in the home such as roundness, sweetness, redness, dog, food, anger, love, mother. He uses these concepts as the tools for thinking. Along with other aspects of intellectual, social, physical, and moral development occurring in middle childhood, the child forms several thousand concepts. If these concepts are true to reality, a good share of them grow out of the child's concrete experience. As he grows older he stores up concepts and becomes able to form new concepts on the basis of vicarious experiences afforded by reading, listening, or seeing films. For example, a considerable amount of research has been done on the development of Havighurst's task, "developing conscience, morality, and a scale of values." Piaget proposes that at birth a child has no conscience and no scale of principles. Values for him are food and warmth. As he learns values and is taught to distinguish between "good" and "bad," the basis for conscience is his parents' punishment combined with acts of love and reward for the child and the child's love and dependence on them. Through the process of identification with parents or taking the role of the parents, the child develops within himself the warning and punishing voice of conscience. From this time on, he carries a controlling force with him wherever he goes. Morality, or a respect for rules and behavior, is imposed first upon the child by the parent. Later, according to Piaget, the child learns the rules that are necessary and useful for playing games or carrying on any human cooperative enterprise. He therefore learns a "morality of cooperation or agreement" which is a true moral autonomy and is necessary in a modern democratic society. Piaget believes that the middle years of childhood are crucial in the development of learning this morality of cooperation. Development of morality and values implies development in an individual of the ability to choose between various objects and modes of action. The growing child must develop a scale of values that will enable him to make stable choices and hold himself to these choices. Piaget (12) has proposed that the development of a scale of values by which a child makes choices proceeds very slowly in the years of middle childhood, but by the age of twelve the child is expected to be more stable in the sense of making a considered choice than he was as a young child seeking immediate satisfaction of every whim.

Much work is being done on the development of moral education by Lawrence Kohlberg who has developed a theory and a program for describing stages of moral development somewhat akin to the kinds of stages which Piaget proposed for all aspects of human development. Kohlberg (8) describes moral development as taking place through three levels which he calls "preconventional, conventional, and autonomous or principled." He proposes that progression through these levels depends on experience and on formal education. He specifically notes that culture teaches the child through interaction with the family, peer group, and other social pressures, such as those within the school, by such means as punishments and rewards, examples by teachers and culture heroes, and other similar influences. Kohlberg proposes that teachers present moral problems and dilemmas to students to encourage effective thinking about moral problems. He suggests that higher moral judgment will result and that the student will develop a solid self-concept which will support him at the level of autonomous and principled moral behavior.

Maslow, Rogers, and other students of human behavior and human development have made similar proposals, but the implications for reading instruction and the impact of reading on the achievement of personal independence and the development of conscience and morality, as well as the impact of reading on other developmental tasks, have been only randomly studied. It seems clear that we need much more longitudinal research of the type done by Loban (9) if we are to understand the ways in which individuals pass through various stages of human development, since each individual passes through the various stages in terms of his own language, culture, and experience in developing a self-concept and a personality.

READING AS AN ASPECT FOR LANGUAGE
Challenging Individual Growth

We know that growth and maturation are continuous processes that go on throughout life. There are periods of time in the development of the individual when the growth is more dramatic and the manifestations of rapid change are more obvious. The years of growth encompassed by the public schools are without question the most dramatic during the period of middle childhood—the intermediate and junior high school years. Grades six, seven, eight, and nine are, almost without exception, the grades in which boys and girls are doing some of the most important growing of their lives. The periods of preadolescence and adolescence have too often been thought of as merely the transitions from stages of childhood to adulthood— periods in which little of importance happens. It may be, as Kohlberg, Piaget, Chomsky, and others are proposing, that growth in all areas of development (physical, social, emotional, mental, and moral) is so rapid during these years that unique individual problems of growth will be more likely to arise. The values, attitudes, and beliefs that young people form during these years are likely to be lifelong and will in large measure determine success or satisfaction. They may determine what the individual will give to or take from life. Therefore, the intermediate school and the junior high have unique functions because they must provide for boys and girls who have unique individual problems. Reading can and should play a vital part in this growth. The reading program must fulfill individual growth functions if it is to provide the kind of experience that will stimulate the individual growth stages. As we have seen in alternative schools, a new curriculum is being formed to include experiences which will stimulate students both in school and out. Instead of deschooling society, society is even more strongly involved in schooling, if not educating children, as Postman and Weingartner have recently noted (13). This fact has lead to an increased search for a viable relationship between school and community in American society. McLuhan's concept of a "classroom without walls" is coming true in many communities. What does this mean for reading?

Materials and Resources

What specific reading materials and resources in the intermediate schools do we need to stimulate the growth and development of preadolescent boys and girls? Many times, certain children stand out as being superior students but we seldom know how superior and in what ways. This is unfortunate if there is truth in the theory that to be really "clever" in the sense that our British colleagues apply the term in education, one has to begin young. Alfred North Whitehead called it a need for "initial momentum." Tutoring took care of John Stuart Mill in this situation: he was taught Greek at the age of three. Michaelangelo, over his father's objection that such work was for artisans, spent his days as a sculptor's apprentice at the age of thirteen and by fifteen shared the company of Lorenzo the Magnificent and his guests, the most able minds in Europe.

Perhaps, with our direction toward alternative schools and classrooms without walls, we will soon be able to apprentice some of our most gifted young people to engineers, artists, or physicists—a challenge which might do a great deal to provide the specific resources in reading that the gifted would need to pursue their special gifts. Malcom X, in his autobiography, points out the development in prison of his own individualized reading program, while he ranged back and forth through classic and contemporary works in the prison library in an effort to find the answer to the dilemma of racial realtionships in our country.

Unfortunately, in most schools we have continued to keep our gifted youngsters studying what they already know and marking time in basic readers in the elementary schools and in required reading courses in English, social studies, and other secondary school programs. Sometimes when they reach for the knowledge they need, they are told to wait; that knowledge will be forthcoming in another book or perhaps in another school. We need more exploration of the known intellectual facets of giftedness such as openmindedness, motivation, tolerance of uncertainty, preference for complexity, high regard for learning, and a sense of destiny. Such criteria are embedded within Havighurst's developmental tasks and demonstrate themselves in classrooms through manifestations of originality, spontaneity, and flexibility as well as the individual's attempts to search for meaning in various situations and to make meanings for himself.

Developmental Psycholinguistics

That a child begins in the very earliest stages of language acquisition to build his own meanings from his own experiences has become within the past several years an important idea in what Frank Smith, Ken Goodman, and others have called developmental psycholinguistics. Although the cooperative work of psycholinguists and reading specialists has become well-known, it is perhaps wise to summarize their definition of reading; this may indicate the kinds of programs and resources we need in schools if we are to develop the abilities of those who are already gifted and further develop additional creative readers throughout the population. In his essay, "Behind the Eye: What Happens in Reading," Goodman (3) gives us the definition of reading which well may serve this purpose:

- Reading begins with graphic language in some form: print, script.
- The purpose of reading is the reconstruction of meaning. Meaning is not in print, but it is meaning that the author begins with when he writes. Somehow the reader strives to *reconstruct* this meaning as he reads.
- In alphabetic writing systems there is a direct relationship between oral language and written language.
- Visual perception must be involved in reading.
- Nothing intrinsic in the writing system or its symbols has meaning. There is nothing in the shape or sequence of any letters or grouping of letters which in itself is meaning.
- Meaning is in the mind of the writer and the mind of the reader.
- Yet readers are capable, through reading, of reconstructing a message which agrees with the writer's intended message.

Reading is a complex process by which a reader reconstructs, to some degree, a message encoded by a writer in graphic language.

Fluent Reading Skills

For the gifted student this search for meaning may be an even more dramatic characteristic of his development than with other children. If one looks only at the development of reading skill, we can say that, by the time that most of the students we classify as gifted reach the intermediate school or junior high, perhaps half find the process of reading to be interesting or rewarding. Many of these children learn to read before they enter the first grade. Many master the encoding/decoding process and are able to use reading either to gain knowledge or for pleasure, perhaps by the age of eight or nine. Nevertheless, a large proportion of children are not stimulated by their elementary school reading programs; and, as we know from the controversies over "individualized reading" and "sequential reading" which were waged during the 1950s, many gifted children are "completely turned off" by the basic reading program. These children respond much more positively to individualized programs, wherein they are able to develop a continuing interest in reading, as well as the skills necessary to use reading for an extension of their own knowledge and for the achievement of various developmental tasks.

In his book *Understanding Reading: A Psycholinguistic Analysis of Reading and Learning to Read*, Smith (16) notes that decoding skills will be of very little use to the reader once he develops what Smith calls *fluent reading*. The development of fluent reading in the gifted child and in all children should be given our highest priority in our new reading program. We need to look carefully at our target before we develop programs and resources. Smith suggests that our target is the development of a child's innate quality as an information processor:

> Man is a creature who devours information. He spends much of his waking time selecting and acquiring information—and a good part of the time he is asleep organizing it.
>
> Man uses all his sensory systems for acquiring information which he integrates and stores in his brain. In the brain, man constructs a model of the world. The model is a summary of all his past experiences and a basis for all his future activity. In fact, it is not possible to separate the past from the future in either the brain or behavior, because in both the ongoing activity reflects past experience and future expectations.
>
> Man's appetite for information can be regarded as a constant search for regularities in external events—regularities that both explain the past and predict the future. The regularities economize on mental effort because they summarize experience and minimize the necessity to remember a multitude of individual events; they provide the basis for rules for deciding when two events should be regarded as being similar or different. Every discovery of a regularity of application of a rule is an instance of uncertainty reduction. As we shall see, the construction of rules for allocating events to a particular category is an important aspect of learning to read.

Smith goes on to point out that the implications of the work of linguists, psycholinguists, and reading specialists who have attempted to study the relationship between language and reading have come to focus on the regularities of language and how a knowledge of them is developed by the child. Essentially, they see reading as an aspect of language, only superficially different from the comprehension of speech, because many of the skills employed by a child in learning the regularities of spoken language may also be employed to learn reading. The basic process, however, is the same. The child attempts to reduce uncertainty and to discover regularity. Smith maintains:

> The point of view just expressed is so different from the way we usually view language perception that it will take a little adjusting to. But we are going to be very deeply involved in the view that reading is not a matter of going from words to meaning, but rather from meanings to words. To read words effectively, you need to have a good idea *in advance* of what it is that you are reading. This is not as paradoxical as it might seem; broadcasters, for example, like to glance through bulletins before they read them because they know it is much easier to enunciate the words appropriately with prior knowledge of the meaning. The question of what meaning actually is, or what comprehension can be, will be approached and then evaded . . . before considering how the receiver might get from raw sound or print to meaning, a function that we have already attributed to grammar.

INDIVIDUALIZATION

This concern for turning reading instruction around so that we start essentially with the individual and his ability to make meanings, rather than with a basic reader in interaction with his environment, is leading us not only to alternatives in the organization of schools and school curriculum but most certainly in reading programs. What are its implications?

Involvement

In *Language and Learning to Read: What Teachers Should Know About Language*, Hodges and Rudorf (*7*) give us the beginning of an answer. They quote the communication model of Ruddell and Bacon (*14*) which encompasses reading, listening, speaking, and writing and focuses on the processes employed by readers and listeners in comprehending oral and written messages: decoding strategies, meaning strategies, and interpretation abilities.

Ruddell and Bacon pay particular attention to the interpretation aspects of the communication model, since they propose that it is by interpretation as a process that the reader (or listener) derives meaning from communication. This process of the derivation of meaning is, they assert, a function of experience, memory, and the skills involved in critical and creative thinking. Taking into account the work of Goodman, Smith, and other linguists and psycholinguists working on the relationship between language and reading, it seems clear that we should be extremely careful in applying such evidence to the development of specific materials and resources for instruction, without duly taking into account the consequences for children.

Further evidence for caution is supplied by Henderson in "Linguistics, Thought, and Reading" (*6*). In his paper, Henderson describes an incident which occurred in a demonstration reading lesson as follows:

> Thirteen or fourteen years ago, I think it was in the spring of 1957, Russell Stauffer taught a demonstration reading lesson with first grade children before a large audience at the University of Pittsburgh. The story was about children who were looking for a penny they had lost while playing in the park. Stopping the readers at this point in the story, Stauffer asked, "How do you think it will end?" All but one child, a boy, agreed that the penny would be found. Then they read to test their prediction. When all were finished, a girl spoke first, "We were right," she said. "They found the penny."
>
> At once the boy who had challenged the prediction ... asked for the microphone and replied, "How do you know it was the same penny?"

"No. We were right," said the girl, "and I can prove it." She turned to the last page of the story and read aloud, "They found the penny." Then she added, "If it had been just any penny, it would have said a penny."

Henderson concludes from this incident that the interplay between language and thinking which exists in the reading process, even in the reading of young children, is so infinitely complex and individualistic that any proposals for resources and materials not developed for specific individuals are simply irrelevant in school reading programs. Particularly with gifted children, we can see this incident multiply itself in depth and complexity in the middle years and we can also see the necessity for resources and materials which develop prediction, hypothesis testing, and substantiation judgment in both younger and older children.

Relevance

We are then presented with a great dilemma in the development of specific materials and resources. If children make up their own meaning and, as Smith and Goodman point out, go from meaning to language rather than language to meaning in learning to read, is it not necessary to provide them with situations both in school and out which will allow them to develop their own meanings in an individually stimulated atmosphere, at least for a part of the school day? Is it not also essential that such development be centered more than ever before on the individual's personal interests as best we can find out about them? Without attempting to be definitive in answering these questions, since I would propose that they merit a great deal more research attention than they have received, I would cite the work of Niles (*10*). In her studies of instructional materials for reading, she has discovered important connections between materials and teachers:

> Many teachers will indicate that they could do a much better job of implementing a reading program if they had better materials. Probably they attach too much importance to materials—good teachers can and often have taught children to read well with very poor materials, even with materials far too difficult for the children. The *sine qua non* is the teacher, not the book.
>
> However, good materials make it easier for the good teacher to do what *could* be done with poorer materials; improvements increase the mileage teachers get from equal expenditures of time and energy. There are three categories of materials to be considered: 1) materials intended specifically for the teaching of reading, 2) library materials, and 3) content area materials. There have never been so many new materials in each of these categories as have flowed from the publishers in the last

two or three years. Two major developments have changed the complexion of many of these materials. The first is the strong emphasis on relevance for today's children and youth. Many teachers feel that difficulty of materials, to which so much attention has been paid in the past, is less important than this relevance. In fact, some feel the lack of relevance may be a major cause of the difficulty. The second trend is toward a multimedia approach.

Relevance is very difficult, if not impossible, to define briefly. We usually think of it as related to interests: a story, for example, is relevant to a group of students if it deals with situations or ideas which they perceive as meaningful and important to them. However, in another sense, materials are relevant if they are expressed in a language which coincides with the language which is familiar to the readers. There has been much discussion of late of the irrelevance, in this sense, of the language of many basal readers. The rationale for the use of the experience approach to early reading depends in part on this matter of relevance of language. Good experience charts are expressed in the actual dialect of the pupils who create and use them.

If we consider the word *relevance* in the way Niles has used it, with special concern for the development of gifted and creative readers, we come ultimately to the question: "What stimulates reading anyway?" If a child is stimulated by relevant materials throughout the years of middle childhood, he may well accomplish all of Havighurst's developmental tasks to a considerable extent and also pass through the various stages of growth noted by Piaget and others. He may come to be the kind of reader that I observed as a commuter moving each day from a suburban community by commuter train to Grand Central Station in New York City. Each morning I would leave at approximately 7:30 a.m., boarding the train with a group of fellow commuters (mostly males), all headed to some job in the center of New York City. My job at the time was at least partially in the field of reading research and also in the development of instructional materials for gifted and creative readers. This was 1963, and we were then at work on the early stages of the *Success in Reading* series (*15*). I began to notice that most of my fellow commuters exhibited a number of characteristics of mature readers as described by Gray and Rogers in their classic study, *Maturity in Reading*. Their reading approach suited their purpose, and the material used was relevant to their purpose. They were usually reading the *New York Herald Tribune*, the *New York Times*, or the *Wall Street Journal*. Their reading patterns were relevant to their developmental tasks. For example, in the case of the *Wall Street Journal*, they would open the paper to the stock market quotations from the previous day, scan until they found the stock they were interested in, and read carefully the opening and closing quotations for the previous day. They would then scan for any stories about stocks that they were interested in on other pages of the paper and do a very careful reading of these stories. They would skim other articles of interest in the paper, and at exactly the time the train reached Grand Central Station at 8:10 they would have done the complete reading job relevant to their purpose. Similar observations were made of readers reading the *New York Times* and the *New York Herald Tribune*. Morning after morning throughout the years of 1962 and 1965, I observed their reading patterns carefully. Similar observations can undoubtedly still be made. Niles might note that relevance for these particular gifted and creative readers existed in the three newspapers.

Relevance to "Saturation"

What about the matter of relevance in specific resources for younger children in the middle years of the intermediate school and junior high? I would cite two further examples: One is that of the experience of Daniel Fader described in *Hooked on Books* and more recently *The Naked Children*. In *Hooked on Books* (1) Fader asks himself:

> But what happens when the materials used in classes for the general student are selected to meet the practical needs of the student rather than the more abstract needs of the subject? In English, for example, rhetoric takes precedence over grammar, and utility becomes more important than beauty. When such criteria become the new basis for selection of materials, a radical change is inevitable. For example, such extremes of the same language as Shakespeare and the daily newspaper are found to have much in common. In terms of the practical needs of the student, the newspaper takes precedence. Because it begins more nearly where he is, it may prove to be the bridge across which he crawls, stumbles and finally walks, erect, to where he should be. If he finds Shakespeare at the other end of the bridge, then the simple, inelegant newspaper, magazine or paperback book has become a legitimate and necessary means to attaining a complex, eloquent end.
>
> When the goal of the English class is redefined in terms of rhetorical ease and willing expression, the ancient methods of the schools become as irrelevant to the subject as they have generally been to the student. Ease in understanding newspapers and pleasure in reading magazines cause both to replace the grammar texts and workbooks of time-dishonored usage. Instead of a student who spells according to rules, we may now have a student who spells by the image of words which have a hundred times impinged on his reading consciousness.
>
> Because the reasons seem as compelling as those for asking teachers *in every classroom* to teach English, the second part of this program is based on the principle of SATURATION, meaning the replacement, whenever possible and in whatever classroom, of customary texts and workbooks with newspapers, magazines and paperbound books. The object of this is to stir the sensibility of the practical child. Even as he learns to be reticent in a world of words he cannot fathom, so may he learn to be receptive in a world of words he can understand. Because he finds newspapers, magazines and paperbound books in every classroom,

and because he *can* and *will* read them, he may yet be brought to compromise with a verbal world he cannot avoid.

Undoubtedly, many of us know the success story of the saturation approach in the Maxey School and in Detroit's Northwestern High School. But these were senior high school students, some might argue; and in some cases they were from socioeconomic and ethnic groups in a rural and an urban community where perhaps some would lack the stimulation of having many books in the home and sharing them with someone who is interested. But saturation and individualization worked here for Fader. Will it work elsewhere? In *How to Survive in Your Native Land*, Herndon (5) tells the story of how he and his two colleagues, Eileen and Arpine, decided to redo the reading program of their school in California. In talking about the seventh and eighth grades, they stated:

> So in the beginning of the school year 1968, we agreed to really teach reading. In the days before school started we—Eileen, Arpine, and I—pooled our combined vast knowledge on that subject. We figured it would be considerable, and indeed it ought to have been considerable. Arpine had never taught before, but she'd just come from courses in reading and children's lit with at least one first-class person at S. F. State; Eileen had already taught reading at a number of different places; I was (since my book came out) a big-shot educator who appeared on TV and was asked to give talks on what was wrong with the schools.
>
> In fact, it soon became clear to us that we didn't know a damn thing for sure. I mean, Eileen knew how to go in there and Teach Reading; she'd done it before and hadn't got killed or anything and she could do it again. Arpine knew a lot of books kids were supposed to like, had heard a lot about motivation, and had read Sylvia Ashton-Warner. All I really had in my head, as it turned out, was that if you got a lot of books around and didn't do anything else, the kids would end up reading them. I also knew that that wasn't true. It might be true in some other situation (like in my head or in someone else's head) but it wasn't true in this particular seventh and eighth grade school which happened to be where we were. One or two kids would read them, one or two kids would write ... in them, one or two kids would throw them, and the rest of the kids would ignore them; that was what would happen right here.
>
> After a couple of days and after a hundred coffees and a thousand cigarettes and a million words and quite a few lunchtime beers we were able to agree that we didn't know nothing. With that we all (I think) quite happily knocked it off, went home for the weekend, and were ready to start.

READING AS AN ART
Capsule Reviewing

After attending a conference with Herb Kohl and others, the three decided to make a complete survey of what was known throughout the field of reading and then to attempt to apply the best that was known and said to their particular students in their school.

> So there, the next year, Arpine and Eileen and I were embarking upon the revolutionary idea that teachers ought to know something about what they were doing. And there was Herb, yet another year and a half later, allowing as how that was so. It amounted to this: *no eye, no hurricane.*
>
> We opened up with testing the kids, determined to try everything once and for all. We had a perfect situation for doing so, for grouping them on the basis of the tests, and for seeing what difference it made, since we were able to test them all individually and handle them in small groups afterwards. We gave an Oral Reading Test, determining from it not only something called Grade Level in reading, but also fitting them into categories according to what kinds of reading difficulties they might be having—i.e., they read well but didn't comprehend, or the reverse; they misread simple words, or inserted words which weren't there, according to context; they had troubles with certain sounds, diphthongs, consonants... we had a checklist of this kind of stuff and followed it through. After a couple of weeks of this we had our eight groups of seven to eight kids apiece, both Arpine and Eileen teaching four periods of reading each, each group about as rightly and rationally and scientifically placed according to grade level and kind of reading problem as you could imagine, short of only having one kid in each group. At the same time we were getting these books out of the library, and consulting with the special reading teacher about what she'd done with many of the same kids last year and getting the district language consultant down with her advice and help with materials and methods, and interviewing salesmen who called on us with this and that workbook, machine, book, classroom magazine or newspaper, drill system, skill developer... we read those pamphlets and books that no one ever looks at, things like *Guidelines to Reading, Reading Development in the Elementary Child, Motivating Reading for the Underachieving Student, The Case for Reading*, the kinds of books held in state college and district education libraries with three authors (the titles of the above are all made up, since who can ever remember them?) and we read Holt and Warner again and we read Tolstoi and I hauled out Bloomfield's marvelous neglected book and we would have read *Reading, Existence and the Absurd, The Zen Method of Reading Improvement*, or *Up Against the Wall Reading Teacher!* if we could have found them (*5*).

Problems of Review

Herndon and his two colleagues, Eileen and Arpine, noted a number of what they call "peculiar things" about the testing. They noticed that many of the students came out much lower on the individual oral test than they did on the schoolwide test, and they also noticed that many of the children who were already gifted and creative readers and who were reading books like *Black Like Me* or Trevor-Roper's books about the Nazis or histories of World War II were pegged by the tests as third or fourth grade level readers. They also noticed that the test was extremely vulnerable to the conscious or unconscious influence of the test-giver on the results; that if the test-giver's job or reputation depended on the improvement of the children, or if the test-giver wanted the children to improve, it was likely that they would improve on the test. There were other problems about the testing, all of which have been written about before. In any case, after a thorough review of current readings in methods and materials proposed for intermediate schools, Herndon and his colleagues came to the following conclusion (5):

> Briefly, we just knew it was absurd that a normal O.K. American kid of any class or kind of twelve years old shouldn't be able to read. Why was it? Because reading is not difficult. Anyone can do it. It is an activity which no one seems to be able to explain but which everyone can do if given a chance. It is simple for people to do. If you know enough to tie your shoe and come in out of the rain, you can do it.
>
> If you can't do it, you must have been prevented from doing it. Most likely what prevented you was teaching. For one thing, if you have to get taught the same "skills" for seven years over and over again, you probably get the notion that it is very difficult indeed. But more important, the "skill" involved in reading is at once very simple and quite mysterious. Once you can look at *c-a-t* and get the notion that it is a clue to a certain sound, and moreover that that very sound which you already know means that particular animal, then you can read, and that is certainly quite simple, even if the ability of humans to do this is opaque. What you probably need to do then is to read a lot and thereby get better at it, and very likely that's what you will do, again, if no one stops you. What stops you is people teaching you skills and calling those skills "reading," which they are not, and giving you no time to actually read in the school without interruption.

Conclusions of Review

What Herndon and his two colleagues were finding out was that their students were having trouble going from print into meaning, instead of from meaning into print. As Herndon himself put it, "They were always practicing up to read, and the practice itself was so unnecessary, or so difficult, or so boring you were likely to figure that the task you were practicing for must combine those qualities and so reject it or be afraid of it." What specific materials and resources then did they decide upon, and what did they find that worked? Not so strongly, Herndon's description (5) sounds very much like that of Fader's "saturation" reading program.

> Somewhere along the way we knew that what we knew about how to teach reading was what our memories could have told us, what we always knew, and that was that reading is best taught by somebody who can already read and who knows and likes the kid—the kid's

mother or father or uncle or tutor or teacher—sitting down with the kid with a book and reading to the kid and listening to the kid read and pointing out things about sounds and words as they go along. That in the past everyone had known how to do that as part of being a parent or an uncle or an older brother and so everyone still knew, if they just wanted to remember it. That the "problem" of reading was simultaneously caused and invented by schools and their insistence on teaching "classes" and "groups"—and by the resulting quest of teachers to find ways to "teach," i.e., ways to standardize and to measure. That there simply is no way to measure what is crucial about reading a book— namely whether or not the kid liked the book, whether he imagined himself involved in the adventures of Jim Hawkins, whether or not he was changed by it. "This should change your life," says Rilke. Who can measure that? And yet it is all that counts.

So we were caught curiously in the middle. We were in a school which hoped to measure and standardize everything, and in which the kids themselves knew that everything important got grades, could be measured, and was standardized. No one was getting A's for being moved to tears when John Silver took off for the last time in the longboat. What we had to do was recreate the way of teaching reading which existed before schools were invented, and use it in the school itself. Reading not as a skill (to be measured), but as an art (that which changes). Nothing could have been simpler. Get a lot of books in the room, tell the kids to bring their own, go around during the period and sit with each kid for a couple of minutes and let him read a bit to you, read some to him perhaps, talk to him about the book and what's going on in it, point out (perhaps) this and that word, sound, and then let him go on and read it while you go over to the next one. Say over and over again—in the classroom, in the teachers' room, in your sleep perhaps—A good reading class is when the kids come in with their books, sit down and read them, and don't stop until the bell rings. Resist the urge to talk and discuss, resist the urge to watch the kids all happily working in the workbooks and programmed materials, resist the urge to motivate and to teach something to everyone at the same time, resist the urge to measure one person against another or everyone against any standard; resist every day all the apparatus of the school which was created in order to enable you to *manage* and *evaluate* a group, since it is just that management which destroyed the kids you have in your class.

Herndon continues saying that the above method works for, as he calls them, his eight, hard-line nonachievers at Rabbit Mountain School as well as it does for the "regulars." He says it works in school terms according to standardized tests, it works in terms of the teacher's observations, and it works in terms of the parents' observations of the students; and to the students' own surprise, since "having battled themselves for so long about reading, they wanted it, when they came to face it, to be a more heroic task."

It worked. I knew it worked because by the end of the first year I stopped hearing all those complaints about reading class. I stopped hearing kids ask me for passes to get out of Reading, to go here and there on some important errand which had to be done during reading period. I stopped hearing about how awful Eileen was and how mean Arpine was. I even heard the dreadful admission that someone was looking forward to going to Reading, looking forward to reading their book, looking forward to a little peace and quiet where they could be left alone and *do what they wanted.*

SUMMARY

There is much more to Herndon's story of **How to Survive in Your Native Land,** but his case study of the teaching of reading in the Rabbit Mountain School may help us to come full circle through the studies of developmental tasks by Havighurst and the work of the developmental psycholinguists, such as Goodman and Smith, to the relevant resources and materials to develop fluent meaning in reading and ultimately to those qualities of giftedness—such as open-mindedness, motivation, tolerance of uncertainty, preference for complexity, high regard for learning, and sense of destiny—present in the creative individual in various dimensions of fluency, originality, spontaneity, and flexibility.

If these are our goals, then we need to change our methods and resources in reading in the ways suggested above. If we are able to do this and to do it soon, we may ensure that passage through the years of middle childhood and adolescence are not merely physical processes but that the social processes involved in Havighurst's developmental tasks become what Friedenberg (*2*) called for more than a decade ago when describing the fundamental task of adolescence as defining "clear and stable self-identification." Friedenberg further pointed out that, if we were able to develop a culture which helped each adolescent begin this definition, we would not be faced with the "pliability" of life in our society and the "dangerous and troublesome prospect" that few youngsters really dare to go through adolescence, that they merely undergo puberty and simulate maturity. It is to the creation of the fully human adolescent—the adolescent who faces life with love and defiance—then, that we need to dedicate our new reading programs and, indeed, our schools as well.

References

1. Fader, Daniel, and Elton B. McNeil. **Hooked on Books.** New York: Berkley, 1966, 16-17.
2. Friedenberg, Edgar Z. **The Vanishing Adolescent.** Boston: Beacon Press, 1959, 2.
3. Goodman, Kenneth S. "Behind the Eye: What Happens in Reading," *Reading: Process and Program*. Champaign, Illinois: Commission on the English Curriculum, National Council of Teachers of English, 1970, 5.

4. Havighurst, Robert J. *Developmental Tasks in Education* (3rd ed.). New York: David McKay, 1972, 19-35.
5. Herndon, James. *How to Survive in Your Native Land*. New York: Bantam Books, 1971, 134-137, 140-141, 143-145.
6. Henderson, Edmund H. "Linguistics, Thought, and Reading," in Richard E. Hodges and E. Hugh Rudorf (Eds.), *Language and Learning to Read: What Teachers Should Know About Language*. Boston: Houghton Mifflin, 1972, 169-188.
7. Hodges, Richard E., and E. Hugh Rudorf. *Language and Learning to Read: What Teachers Should Know About Language*. Boston: Houghton Mifflin, 1972, 169-188.
8. Kohlberg, Lawrence, and Turiel Elliot. "Moral Development and Moral Education," in Gerald Lesser (Ed.), *Psychology and Educational Practices*. Chicago: Scott, Foresman, 1971, 139-145.
9. Loban, Walter. *Problems in Oral English: Kindergarten Through Grade Nine*. Champaign, Illinois: National Council of Teachers of English, 1966.
10. Niles, Olive S. "School Programs: The Necessary Conditions," *Reading Process and Program*. Champaign, Illinois: Commission on the English Curriculum, National Council of Teachers of English, 1970, 66-67.
11. Piaget, Jean. *The Language and Thought of the Child*. Leuchatel-Paris: Delachaux and Niestle, 1923.
12. Piaget, Jean. *The Moral Judgment of the Child*. New York: Harcourt, Brace and World, 1932, 55.
13. Postman, Neil, and Charles Weingartner. *The Schoolbook*. New York: Delacorte Press, 1973.
14. Ruddell, Robert B., and Helen G. Bacon. "The Nature of Reading: Language and Meaning," in Richard E. Hodges and E. Hugh Rudorf (Eds.), *Language and Learning to Read: What Teachers Should Know About Language*. Boston: Houghton Mifflin, 1972, 169-188.
15. Shafer, Robert et al. *Success in Reading*, Volumes 1-8. Morristown, New Jersey: Silver Burdett, General Learning Corporation, 1973.
16. Smith, Frank. *Understanding Reading: A Psycholinguistic Analysis of Reading and Learning to Read*. New York: Holt, Rinehart and Winston, 1971, 28, 34-35.

CREATIVITY TRAINING ACTIVITIES FOR SECONDARY SCHOOL STUDENTS

Joseph S. Renzulli
and
Carolyn M. Callahan
University of Connecticut

Although research has consistently shown that almost all students can improve the quantity and quality of their creative output, many secondary school teachers experience a great deal of difficulty when they attempt to encourage youngsters to express themselves creatively. Part of this difficulty is due to group pressures toward conformity that typically exist among adolescents, but the problem is also a result of our failure to teach students the basic skills of creative thinking. All too often we have assigned students higher-level creativity tasks without first providing them with the underlying techniques that are necessary for more complicated assignments such as writing expressive poetry, creative stories, or imaginative essays. The purpose of this chapter is to point out some of the basic techniques for encouraging youngsters to think creatively. The first part of the chapter will deal with the general strategies for developing creativity training activities. This will be followed by brief descriptions of some specific activities that can be used to give students practice in creative thinking.

PRINCIPLES UNDERLYING CREATIVITY TRAINING

The Fluency Principle

Research in creativity training has shown that the more ideas a person generates, the more likely he is to come up with new and unusual ideas. For example, when a group of students was presented with the hypothetical problem of thinking up a name for a new breakfast cereal made from dandelions, almost all of the students called the cereal "Dandy Flakes." Since creative ideas are, by definition, unusual or infrequent solutions to problems, and since "Dandy Flakes" was the response given by more than 90 percent of the students, it was judged to be a relatively common response. The teacher then asked the students to think of five more possible names for the new breakfast cereal. Needless to say, several unusual names were created; and in many cases, students developed names that were unique to the group. For example, one student suggested manufacturing the cereal in the shape of lions or lions' heads and then calling the cereal "Dandy Lions."

This example helps to illustrate the fluency principle. Unless we encourage students to develop many ideas rather than just one, and unless we reward them for the sheer quantity of ideas they produce, they may never get beyond the ordinary and the obvious. Fluency training activities such as the dandelion problem give students practice in the basic creativity technique of brainstorming. Such activities are good warm-up exercises for more complicated activities because they help youngsters explore various alternatives to problems and thereby free their thinking processes from the restraints that usually hinder creativity.

The Principle of Open-endedness

The principle of open-endedness is closely related to the fluency principle. Simply stated, it means that creativity training exercises should not have predetermined answers. A good deal of the "education game" that is played between teachers and students is based on the mental process of convergence. Teachers usually raise problems that have one predetermined solution and students are rewarded for the speed and accuracy with which they converge on the solution. Such exercises provide students with very limited opportunities to let their minds reach across a broad range of possible solutions to a given problem.

Open-ended activities also help students develop the skills of self-evaluation. When an answer is either right or wrong, the final source of judgment always resides with an external authority—usually the teacher or a textbook. With the threat of evaluation and the fear of being wrong constantly hanging over their heads, it is little wonder that students are reluctant to take risks and to express thoughts and ideas that are somewhat unusual or divergent. Open-ended activities, on the other hand, provide youngsters with a psychologically safe atmosphere in which to express themselves. When there are no right or wrong answers to problems, and when students are given an opportunity to generate many possible solutions to a particular problem, a situation is created that enables students to review their own alternative responses and to select the response that they like best. This is not to say that the teacher and other students should not have an opinion about a youngster's work.

But the important thing to keep in mind is that the student himself has passed judgment on his own work and that his opinion is a valid one because it is based on his own standards and criteria for self-satisfaction.

Open-ended activities such as the dandelion problem can be used to create an atmosphere where students can develop free and open thinking without the usual restraints that frequently result from rigorous external evaluation. We can help youngsters become more creative thinkers by giving them numerous opportunities to practice on material which allows for many acceptable responses and then by allowing them to bring their own judgmental processes to bear on the responses they produce.

The Principle of Environmental Relevancy

When students are engaged in creativity training, they should not be penalized for a lack of knowledge about a particular topic. In other words, creativity training activities should allow the learner to draw upon his own background and experiences. For example, if we asked youngsters to engage in "thing listing" by writing all of the things they might find in a kitchen, they would not have to search through reference books in order to make several responses. Because this is an open-ended exercise that is based on experiences that are relatively common to all youngsters, it also helps to make adjustments for differences in background and ability level. Youngsters from affluent homes might list luxury items such as garbage disposals and microwave ovens, but even students from so-called disadvantaged homes will be able to respond within the limits of their own experience. And while less able students are likely to focus mainly on concrete items, brighter students may include certain intangibles, such as pleasant aromas and the warm atmosphere that they might associate with a kitchen.

As has been indicated above, the major purpose of warm-up activities is to give students practice in generating several ideas and solutions to a given problem. Unless these activities are relevant to a student's present background and immediate environment, the exercises are likely to become traditional search-for-information experiences. The major purpose of developing brainstorming skills can easily be lost if the student is asked to slow down divergent thinking processes in order to search out factual information. Thus, it is important in creativity training to develop exercises that are based on information that is relatively common to all members of a group and, at the same time, to select activities that are open-ended and that allow for many responses.

The Principle of Enjoyment

Creativity training, like any other aspect of the teaching-learning process, can become a routine and dreary experience if we do not guard against the forces that tend to stifle enthusiasm and enjoyment. Even the most exciting activities can lose their appeal if they are administered in a mechanical fashion by teachers who are not enthusiastic. One of the best ways a teacher can demonstrate her genuine interest in creativity is to become an active participant in training activities. When the teacher shows a willingness to reveal her own creative thoughts and ideas, when she contributes to class discussions on an equal basis with students, and when she is not afraid to operate in a free and open atmosphere, students will quickly develop trust in the teacher and security in situations where unusualness is rewarded rather than punished. It is one thing to tell students that we want them to strive for originality and "way out" solutions to open-ended problems, but it is much more effective to achieve trust by actually displaying the kind of behavior that the teacher is attempting to elicit from students.

Whenever teachers and students are purposefully striving for unusualness, a good deal of laughter and humor is likely to be displayed. It is important for the teacher to be accepting of these reactions (especially laughter directed at the teacher's creative ideas) because humor is an important part of creativity. Attempts to suppress laughter will invariably result in a dampening of the free and open atmosphere that is necessary for the development of uninhibited expression.

Students will also derive more enjoyment from creativity training sessions if they have an opportunity to participate in planning the activities. While we hear a great deal of talk about cooperative planning, much of what goes on in classrooms is solely determined by the teacher. Once students have been exposed to a variety of creativity training exercises, they should be given a choice about which types of activities they would like to pursue. Since the objective of such activities is the development of creative thinking processes rather than coverage of subject matter, creativity training exercises provide an opportunity for students to deal with topics that are of interest to them. For example, adolescents can practice brainstorming by listing all of the possible names they can think of for musical rock groups. If students are interested in politics or ecology, they may want to write slogans or design symbols that promote their points of view. Capitalizing upon student interests will help to maintain enjoyment and enthusiasm and, at the same time, will shorten the communication gap that often exists between adolescents and their teachers.

CREATIVITY TRAINING ACTIVITIES
Creative Writing

As has been indicated, creativity training exercises are designed to help free students from the usual constraints that are placed on their thinking and thus prepare them for higher level assignments such as creative writing. Numerous activities can be developed around brainstorming and thing-listing formats. In preparation for creative writing, students can develop lists of words that are related to given emotions such as fear, happiness, and sadness. They can also be given the stems of common similes such as "as big as _____" and "as quiet as _____" and asked to develop several colorful comparisons that will complete each simile. Similar exercises can be developed for analogies and metaphors. In each case, it is important for students to generate as many responses as possible for each item. Students can also be asked to apply the brainstorming technique to developing lists of synonyms and antonyms for given words. Additional word fluency exercises can be carried out by asking students to write specific ways of conveying a certain meaning. For example, there are several dozen specific ways of communicating the act of speaking (say, bellow, whine, mumble), each with its own special meaning. Students will gain greater control over their writing when they learn to explore a wide variety of possible words to create a certain mood or feeling.

Word-listing activities can be used to help prepare students for writing poetry. Prior to introducing rhyming patterns in poetry, students can be asked to list all of the words they can think of that rhyme with a given word. This exercise will generate a great deal of excitement if carried out under mildly competitive conditions. Students can compete individually or in groups to see who can develop the longest lists of rhyming words. After they have completed their lists, they can be introduced to rhyming patterns such as those used in limericks and asked to use words from their lists to write original limericks.

One of the problems that teachers often face when attempting to develop creative writing abilities is helping students generate interesting ideas for their stories. Brainstorming and thing-listing exercises can be used to assist students in the process of idea finding. For example, students can be asked to list ten or twelve roles or characters in the first of four columns on a piece of paper. Each item should be numbered. Characters or roles might include spacemen, hippies, and deep sea divers. The second column should contain a list of places: the inside of a fallout shelter, a jungle, an underwater cave. The third list should contain actions: swimming, building an igloo, chopping down a tree. The final column should contain objects: teapot, television antenna, broom. After all of the lists have been completed, the students should randomly select one item from each list by rolling a set of dice or using a spinner. The items selected from each of the four lists should then be used as the elements for a short story. Forcing relationships among things that may not logically be related may result in the creation of some interesting and unusual stories. Students can use their lists several times, and the activity can be varied by placing certain specifications on one or more of the lists. For example, the list containing characters might be restricted to famous people or characters that students have encountered in their reading. The actions list can be restricted to occupations or recreational activities, and similar kinds of restrictions can be placed on the lists of things and places.

A similar technique can be used to help students develop interesting character sketches. Categories of physical characteristics such as weight, height, age, eyes, hair, and build can be written on a piece of paper. Students should be asked to list as many words or phrases as they can think of under each category. For example, under the age category, students might list *baby, girl, teenager, old man*. After students have listed as many words as they can under each heading, one item should be randomly selected from each list and the words used as the basis for a character sketch. Needless to say, some unusual and quite fanciful characters will emerge from this technique; however, it will help students break away from the formula type of characters that often result when students are not given practice in combining characteristics that are sometimes incongruous. The main purpose of this technique is to help youngsters stretch their imaginations by providing them with an exercise where unusual relations are forced together.

The brainstorming and word-listing techniques can also be used to help students develop the skills of descriptive writing. Students can be asked to list all of the words they can think of that are associated with each of the five senses. For example, under the sense of touch, they might include *smooth, rough, mushy*. After students have completed their lists, they can be asked to write descriptive paragraphs that highlight some of the words on their lists. The paragraphs might focus on one of the senses or a combination of two or more senses. Students can also be asked to brainstorm a number of topics for description—a rainy afternoon or the midway at a carnival—and then write a description that incorporates perspectives on the topic from each of the five senses.

Figural and Symbolic Creativity Activities

One way of capitalizing on student interests and special talents is to combine figural and symbolic activities with verbal activities. For example, students might be asked to design a camper or a recreation park using given size specifications. When the designs have been completed, a number of verbal exercises are natural follow-up activities. Students might be asked to write slogans to sell the camper, a technical description of the park that would be sufficient for the landscaper to lay out the park, a classified ad for the camper, a political speech that would convince the town council to provide the funds to build the recreation park, or even a simple description of the camper or recreation park. One might also make use of special interests in art or music by asking students to write descriptions of moods created by abstract paintings or music played on a tape recorder or record player.

The close connection between symbols, emotions, and propaganda might be the basis for a thing-listing activity in which students are presented with pictures of well-known symbols such as the peace symbol, hammer and sickle, star of David, or United Nations symbol. They may then be asked to write a list of their emotional responses, followed by an essay on how these symbols have been or might be used for propaganda purposes.

The use of an activity where students can create closely related verbal slogans and symbols for a business, club, or school team will often motivate the child with little verbal fluency but some artistic ability to complete a verbal task by its close association with a symbolic task. It is, of course, important that the teacher reward both efforts in order to emphasize the need for a fluency of modes of expression as well as fluency within a given mode of expression.

SUMMARY

There are a number of general techniques for encouraging youngsters to think creatively. The four basic principles underlying creativity training have been discussed. By way of summary the fluency principle states that the more ideas a person generates, the more likely he is to come up with new and original ideas. Open-endedness implies that creativity training exercises should not have predetermined answers; instead they should enable students to generate many solutions to a given problem. Environmental relevancy emphasizes that students should not be penalized for lack of knowledge about a particular topic. The principle of enjoyment suggests that enthusiasm is an important part of creativity and that a free and open atmosphere is necessary for the development of uninhibited expression.

These principles and the specific suggestions which followed were not intended as cookbook recipes for creative thinking or as formulas which in and of themselves will lead to the creation of brilliant literary works. However, the principles and the activities which develop from them do serve a very important function in the development of the creative thinking processes. They free the student from the traditional modes of thinking which call for him to search for the one right solution and, instead, encourage him to explore many possible alternative responses, draw upon his entire life experience in searching for responses, evaluate his own responses, and enjoy and feel confident in expressing his ideas to others no matter how real or unreal, true or fanciful, practical or whimsical, those ideas might be.

PART FOUR

SUGGESTIONS FOR MEETING UNIQUE NEEDS

One of the greatest potential sources of gifts and talents waiting to be tapped is the gifted child who, as measured by the standard norm, differs in clothing, dialect, or culture. To develop these gifts and talents we must provide learning experiences which reflect the values and make use of the real language of these pupils for whom *suggestions for meeting unique needs* are made.

Growth will occur as each child participates comfortably in understanding how language works for him and for others. Furthermore, by understanding his own interests, concerns, purposes, and extent of development he will be dealing with the essence of reading.

Motivation for meeting the unique needs of certain gifted and creative students may be accomplished through many avenues. One important training approach is called "make-believe." As the child tries and tests various ideas (as suggested in Part IV), his feelings of others—both real and fanciful—are brought into focus through activities in art, rhythm, dramatization, and creative writing.

Educational problems that may lead to decline rather than growth are also discussed. Of particular importance are problems which are attributable to lack of educational reform, misleading ideas that gifted children do not need special assistance, and the immature mores of all parties concerned. These unique children are hindered in maintaining respect for individual variabilities, thus encouraging failure in learning. To prevent this failure, the needs of early and older readers are pointed out and a variety of reading programs and techniques are suggested. Ninety-five challenging enrichment activities are suggested for providing powerful instruments of learning in developing this unique, creative reader.

This section also focuses on putting positive theory into practice and thereby allowing equal emphasis for minority group, learning disabled, gifted, and creative children. The needs of this diverse, creative group are outlined. The schools overcome lack of success by developing the strong points in the special child rather than focusing on what is weak and lacking in him. Finally, this section offers a number of activities that have been used successfully with children who are classified as being different.

M.L.

MAKE-BELIEVE: AN IMPORTANT AFFAIR

Margaret S. Woods
Seattle Pacific College

"What do you believe in?" each youth asks as he grows to manhood. The answers which satisfy the youth may vary considerably, and he will ask for reasons. His acceptance of those reasons will depend upon feelings gained from his own experiences and upon authorities in whom he has come to believe as a result of those experiences. Among the earliest training events for every child, especially for the gifted child, are situations in which the child is enabled to make-believe, to try out various ideas, and to test both his own feelings and the feelings others express about both real and fanciful worlds.

During a 200-year period, Toynbee postulated (7), a great nation moves

>From Bondage to Spiritual Faith
>From Spiritual Faith to Great Courage
>From Great Courage to Liberty
>From Liberty to Abundance
>From Abundance to Selfishness
>From Selfishness to Complacency
>From Complacency to Apathy
>From Apathy to Dependence
>From Dependence back again to Bondage.

We might conjecture, "Just suppose monies which go into financing and launching a rocket were allocated instead for launching into life's orbit fully equipped human rockets always ready to operate to prevent malfunctioning at any stage." *Just suppose*—two words which help us to see the world as it is, to imagine what it might be like, and then, hopefully, to possess the courage to change. According to Toynbee, one who learns how to use his power to create is free at any time to save the situation by developing new techniques, new institutions, new ideas, new attitudes of mind, and, above all, new states of feeling.

We are rapidly approaching a crisis time when the efforts of all must yield new answers. There will be a demand for creative individuals to practice their skills of creating. This author contends that such skills are learned from many instances of "just supposing," or "making believe."

THE MEANING OF MAKE-BELIEVE

That powerful catalyst, *imagination*, has been recognized by teachers as the source which supplies the well-oiled machinery for maximizing the individual's potential. Einstein considered imagination to be more important than knowledge. Anatole France said, "To imagine is everything; to know is nothing at all." Holbrook (3) concluded that nourishment and exercise of imagination are the roots of true literacy in all, from low stream to genius.

Trevisa defined the power that we call imagination as the "Faculty for forming Images whereby the Soul beholdeth the Likeness of Things that be Absent" (1). Frye (2) defined imagination as "an unborn or embryonic belief."

Observing children at play, a teacher can usually recognize *imagination* at work in all make-believe activities, which Isaacs (4) called "Nature's means of individual education." Through the use of make-believe, children are able to discover what life appears to be through active participation; they investigate the world of society through a mental experiment, Scarfe's definition (6) of make-believe.

Make-believe may be called the magic of the mind which enables children to give concentrated attention to isolated elements in their real or imagined worlds. As they wrestle with problems of their own worlds of work and play, they increase their powers of accurate observation, their sensitivity to implications, and their awareness of multiple causations. They develop the power to create as their understandings improve. As they encounter the world of literature, they are able to envision the many possibilities suggested by a description or an incident.

Make-believe is, first of all, a source of hope—hope for a solution, for something better. It makes possible, with safety, an integration of feelings, needs, and interests with subject matter. A child can handle situations with a combination of ease and effort, proceeding to new ideas as he validates existing ideas and finds them comfortable. In a climate in which he feels both safe and free, he will engage in the highly personal business of revealing himself and his ideas to others.

Each make-believe experience is characterized by a freshness, an involvement of the whole being in the discovery process which ensues. Krishnamarti (5) stated that discovery is the beginning of creativeness and that without creativeness, do what we may, there can be no peace nor happiness for man.

MAKE-BELIEVE ACTIVITIES

For the past twenty years, there has existed a cooperative venture in which parents and public libraries have supported the serious business of make-believe through an action program. The community-sponsored series, "Let's Pretend with the Fours and Fives," has placed emphasis on the carryover into everyday life of the following values absorbed through identification with storybook characters: confidence, curiosity, courage, humor, understanding, persistence, patience, honesty, loyalty, compassion, thoughtfulness, awareness, and hope.

From such programs have come the following suggestions for utilizing make-believe for individual education:

1. To give children the courage "to be" and "to become," have them enact a scene similar to this: Pretend to be rabbits crouched behind an imaginary fence, eyeing Mr. McGregor's every move, waiting for his watchful eye to disappear, giving the signal that it is safe to wriggle under the fence.
2. To eliminate unpleasant situations, set limits within which children will sense the need for safety to operate: "Let's find a place for turning our rope so that it will not bump anybody" allows freedom, sets standards, and establishes a precedent for future actions.
3. To provide a rich source of satisfaction in "being the cause of" something which is ultimately, if not almost immediately, successful, guide a child so that he will understand what caused his success: Have him move into an imaginary garden as Peter Rabbit, making absolutely no sound. A successful child will say something like, "You know, my feet were so quiet I couldn't even hear them myself."
4. To develop techniques suitable for personal use, permit each child to experiment: Honor the child's request to "let me do it my different way."
5. To open inspiration channels, encourage verbalization of impressions: Ask children what they think should happen; have them act out one another's ideas.
6. To help children gain insight into the "secret self" of another person, provide viewing experiences: Let a shy child observe other children pretending to be Mr. McGregor. Eventually, the shy youngster may say, "I bet now I could be Mr. McGregor and scare 'em out, huh?"

7. To capitalize on intellectual vigor and creative spirit, provide repetitive experiences: Have children plan what they will do next time. A five-year-old may suggest, "Next time, let's build an electric fence! Boy, that will pull all the hair out of the rabbits!"
8. To help children see what human beings are really like, have them pretend to be mother, father, teacher, neighbor, or an animal: Suggest actions or situations that will develop insight into the ways characters behave.
9. To enable children to face fearful situations, guide them through essential steps: "Talk a child through" Little Red Riding Hood's walk to Grandmother's house, taking one possibility at a time so that the child has courage for each step.
10. To make it possible for a child to assume a real-life role at a later time, have him pretend: Create a scene in a hospital emergency room, and have children act out the roles of attendants, doctors, and patients.
11. To aid children in acquiring values, have them act out roles of characters who crusade for justice, goodness, and freedom: Select a familiar fairy tale character, and let children dramatize an episode from the tale.

SUMMARY

Make-believe—the result of utilizing one's imagination to create a way to handle a situation—enables the individual to practice various skills of creating and to attain an ability to create in time of need. Suggestions for utilizing make-believe for individual education include a variety of activities in which children enact scenes, recognize limits, acknowledge causes of success, experiment with techniques, verbalize impressions, view the efforts of others, repeat scenes with variations, assume various roles, experience emotions, act out real-life scenes, and dramatize fairy tale characters.

References

1. Cane, Florence. *The Artist in Each of Us.* New York: Pantheon Books, 1951.
2. Frye, Northrop. *The Educated Imagination.* Bloomington, Indiana: Indiana University Press, 1964.
3. Holbrook, David. *English for the Rejected.* London: Cambridge University Press, 1964.
4. Isaacs, Susan. *The Nursery Years.* New York: Schocken Books, 1968.
5. Krishnamarti. *Seattle and King County Libraries Newsletter.* Seattle, Washington: 1953.
6. Scarfe, Neville. "Play in Education," unpublished lecture given at the University of British Columbia.
7. Woods, Margaret S. "Are You Creative or Computerized?" *Overview*, University of Washington Student Teacher Journal, 1972.

CREATIVE READING CAN BE A BALANCE AND AN ANCHOR IN GUIDING THE GIFTED

Ann F. Isaacs
National Association for Gifted Children
Cincinnati, Ohio

It is small wonder that the plight of the gifted child evokes little understanding or sympathy. Most parents do not know when their children are gifted, and teachers do not recognize the gifted in their classrooms. More than half of the school administrators think there are no such childen in their schools (20). In the literature in education and psychology, the gifted child is seldom mentioned; when there is discussion, the difficulties of being gifted are rarely emphasized.

It should be apparent that conflicts may arise at some stage of the gifted child's interaction with others, simply because the child's expectations and/or responses will differ from those of other children and hence will not seem appropriate or normal in the situation. It is the purpose of this chapter to explore some of the problems and to suggest procedures related to reading instruction that may reduce or eliminate conditions detrimental to gifted children.

SPECIAL NEEDS OF GIFTED CHILDREN
Possible Educational Problems

Some gifted children learn to read during their preschool years. A common fact, one rarely noted in the educational literature, is the tragic way these precocious learners fare. Instead of working in their favor, the advanced beginning can prove to be a negative achievement since many teachers, although skilled in many ways, do not know how to cope with the five-year-old who reads.

Children who are able to read at the beginning of their first year of school may later show a decline rather than growth in reading. Thus, children who enter school reading unhaltingly may begin to read falteringly. These children face a combination of negatives: A teacher whose attitudes may range from passivity to hostility, plus a peer group from whom they are often isolated because their superior reading abilities do not create an emotional climate in which excellent reading carries positive overtones. Consequently, punishment rather than reward is the reinforcement which early readers tend to receive.

Literature on the gifted may be misleading because it may tend to stress achievements and fail to mention the gifted child's problems. Not uncommonly he is in need of remediation in reading. Many gifted children have been known to read several levels below their potential, a fact which would make average children candidates for remediation. When it is realized that the gifted should be able to read several levels above grade placement, their problems when regarded in proper perspective, loom even larger than do the problems of average children (*15*).

Thus, many gifted children who should be receiving help remain unaided because their performance is acceptable when compared with the average. It is only when the underachievement is viewed within the range of what fellow gifted children with similar mental endowments are achieving that the true extent of these children's needs becomes apparent.

The beautiful part about helping the gifted child overcome a problem is that, with good rapport and constructive remediation, a teacher can be rapidly rewarded and find the time spent exceedingly worthwhile. With good achievement, the gifted child no longer requires additional time and effort from the teacher; he rapidly becomes an asset and aid to all classroom endeavors.

Some teachers take the attitude that parents of the gifted are too aggressive. Still others are ready to state that all parents think their children are gifted. These ideas are greatly in contrast to the facts, at least within the writer's experience. More often the reverse is true; parents are highly hesitant about calling their children gifted and do so only with the greatest reluctance.

Many parents are more than willing to "explain away" a child's superiority. They will attribute achievement to the influence of an older sibling or to time spent with the child or to extra experience or to television. It will be noted that teachers are no more knowledgeable. They, too, are eagerly willing to suggest that any child could achieve similarly, given suitable opportunities.

It is unfortunate that a nonachieving gifted child frequently is unidentified and neglected. The child thus experiences personal suffering when functioning below his potential because he senses that he should be performing at a higher level. This loss is ours as well, for if any one of us is diminished, we all are diminished. The greatest loss, of course, is that the far-reaching potential of the gifted child may never be realized.

Young parents who bring a gifted child to his first school experience need encouragement. Instead, they may be confronted with the first of a long series of battles as the child encounters new teachers. These boys and girls are so different from neighbor children that their precocious qualities may be evaluated negatively, rather than positively, with the child being ostracized from play with peers. At times, a parent has no way of knowing that his child's behavior is on a superior level. In some cases a majority of children in a given neighborhood may be gifted. The result may be that giftedness in such a situation is perceived as the norm, and again not properly valued.

The Needs of Gifted Early Readers

Durkin (*5*) found that early readers hold the gains they have made. She followed up the superior reader who arrived in school reading and found that, when compared six years later with other students of the same mental age, the superior ones had maintained their lead.

Isaacs (*13*) points out that early reading is not necessarily advisable for all gifted children. However, children who do read at an early age need to be encouraged by these measures:

1. Permit the child to read with children in higher grades.
2. Give the child opportunities to work with an outside consultant.
3. Enable the child to pursue other activities suggested by the consultant.
4. Excuse the child from routine library assignments.
5. Encourage other activities suggested by the librarian.
6. Permit the child to receive help from older students and to give help to younger students in other grades.
7. Encourage task-sharing with the child's own classmates.
8. Request other teachers to permit the child to share his ideas with their classes.
9. Permit the child to help in the role of teacher's aide.
10. Arrange suitable grade placement, even if this requires skipping grades.
11. Promote writing of the child's own stories.
12. Allow time for dramatizing and directing the enactment of poems, stories, and plays.

It is a commonly held notion that most gifted children learn to read by themselves. (The author's experience suggests that, while most may be able to recognize words or phrases, only very few are fluid independent readers.) Those who know gifted preschool children casually may believe that the children are reading fluidly and excellently. Frequently, however, what passes for reading, is the love of books. Often the gifted child's superior memory makes him appear to be reading. Close observation will reveal that he is more often turning the pages and reciting from memory.

For the gifted child, reading can be both balance and anchor. Reading gives perspective to his visions of who he is and who he might become. Reading opens up imaginary vistas which can, in maturity, become reality. The child whose environment is repeatedly circumscribed with limitations may find reading to be the magic carpet to the future and to the treasures of the world. A child's life at the moment may be impoverished, but the vast vistas to the future which reading opens can provide the proper springboard. To this child, the present becomes more acceptable in light of what the future may bring.

The Needs of Older Gifted Children

In contrast to popular opinion, many gifted children have reading problems. Careful diagnosis will reveal that they suffer some of the same emotional-psychological problems as do nongifted groups. In addition, they have unique problems induced by their giftedness and attendant problems which may be characterized as psychosociological.

Teachers and principals sometimes mistakenly feel that helping gifted children regress to the norm is desirable, and they do their best to make this happen. It should be clear that children who first read several levels above grade placement, and then regress to grade level or below, are striving for social approval and are more eager to gain peer acceptance than to maintain their superior position as better readers.

Ability to excel is based on superior endowment and does not necessarily insure the development of efficient study skills (*19*). When parents and teachers discover deficiencies in a child's reading, problem sources need to be identified and eliminated.

In a conference, an eight-year-old boy (153 IQ on the revised LM Stanford-Binet Intelligence Scale) revealed how he and fellow classmates coped with boredom in the regular classroom. Although he was in the top reading group in his second grade, he confided that he had read the book they were using sixteen times. Was he then permitted to remain in his seat when his group was called? "Oh, no," he said. "Everyone has to go when the group is called except those who go to the bathroom."

"Do you mean those who *had* to go to the bathroom?"

"Well, some had to go. But others went to swing on the bars. Then, by the time they got back to the room, the reading group was half or two-thirds over."

(One wonders how the student knew this unless he too had been in the bathroom during his own reading-group time.)

WAYS TO GUIDE GIFTED CHILDREN IN AND THROUGH READING

Individualized Programs

Permitting a gifted child to remain in his seat pursuing books of his own choice is a simple modification of individualized reading. This is the least difficult approach for the teacher and the one most appropriate for children who do not need the typical reading group. Books may be brought from home or selected from the library by the teacher or the child.

The individualized, personalized approach to reading has been successful when used by competent practitioners. Barbe (*3*), Witty (*14*), Duker (*4*), Spalding (*18*), and Williamson (*21*) are all in accord concerning the value of this mode of teaching reading. Gifted children especially derive these benefits:

1. Proceed at their own pace.
2. Develop a positive relationship with the teacher.
3. Experience success and improved self-esteem.
4. Be responsible for their own reading.
5. Have freedom in the selection of materials.
6. Discuss their reading with someone.

The advantages of individualized reading are many, the following being most important for gifted children and their teachers:

1. The program enables the teacher to meet the needs of each child.
2. Conferences and reports provide a means for diagnosis.
3. The teacher has time to spend with individual children at critical moments.
4. The teacher can provide a carefully structured program to develop skills.
5. The teacher attains a higher degree of job satisfaction.
6. The teacher becomes a director of learning.

Linguistics Study

Marckwart (*16*) investigated today's various trends of linguistic study. Some of the attributes of the gifted which are overtly apparent (excellent retention, large vocabulary, deep and varied interests, intense curiosity, great persistence, and high IQ) make the study of linguistics highly appealing. Researchers may focus on particular elements, such as phonology, morphology, accent, syntax, semantics, and/or grammar.

Creative Reading Programs

Creative reading is the highest type and most neglected reading skill. Typically, reading is taught with "note the details and central thought" approach. The creative reader is capable of divergent responses rather than convergent ones. The creative reader possesses the ability to examine relationships among facts and interpretations.

The extent of children's interest in reading and the number of books read may provide clues to giftedness. But without guidance, creative reading may never happen. Materials which are randomly selected, even when voraciously pursued, will not provide maximum benefits to a child. Reading rate and comprehension may grow, but the motivation for reading may remain at the escape level rather than proceed to the mature growth and insight level.

Books can transport the reader to imaginary ports which are never seen in reality. This purpose of stirring the imagination is not to be denied nor demeaned. Reading also contains the power of helping children realize who they are and, more importantly, who they can hope to become.

Creative reading can be fostered by making available all kinds of good books. Children are helped by having the opportunity to become more critical and more self-directing. They can be encouraged to demonstrate their reactions and interpretations through laughing, crying, and recounting, and even to change their language patterns through conscious effort (*2*).

Learning to read critically but constructively, and rewriting what does not appeal, can improve both critical and creative abilities. The same approach can be used to gain a higher order of involvement and application from the gifted as they are introduced to various forms of literature (*6*). This is in keeping with one of the goals of helping the gifted gain mastery of communication skills, enabling them to share their talents.

Self-acceptance can grow as a result of positive experiences and rewarding creative efforts. Underachievers have often been found to be self-rejecting, but they too can have opportunities to create. Pilon (*17*) suggests picture books as tools for building confidence in nonreaders.

Flexible Language Arts Programs

Flexibility in reading instruction for advanced students is an excellent mode of meeting individual needs (*7*). Progress is enhanced by good teaching, and fundamental skills still need to be given attention, sometimes at a faster pace. Learning prefixes, suffixes, and combining forms can increase vocabulary and materially aid both oral and written communication (*12*). Grade levels should not set the limits, and both classwork and individual assignments should be flexible. In addition, books, audiotapes, filmstrips, programed learning materials, magazines, newspapers, and weekly scholastic papers are helpful. Gifted children are also especially fond of crossword puzzles, folk and fairy tales, science reading, and new books which receive annual recognition through the Newbery and Caldecott Awards.

A sensitive teacher can provide practice opportunities for leadership and responsibility for the gifted. Simultaneously, the gifted child can be striving for further giftedness by gaining ability to give psychological comfort, being willing to teach others, and striving for high ideals and good judgment.

Both children and adults agree that there are times when a teacher can best serve a gifted student by leaving him alone. There is need, however, for providing sources to which the student may refer, such as school personnel, the library, or lists of activities.

Bibliotherapy

Many gifted children, both contemporary and emeritus, have confided in the author that they knew they were "different," but that they were never able to decide whether this difference was good or bad. A mature student in this field may conclude that the child suffered from a confused role-concept or faced an identity crisis. Although giftedness is ideally used for the good of all, it can be detrimental to society as well as painful to the individual. Helping a child understand giftedness is one of the most important roles an adult can fill, whether the child is already functioning at the gifted level or is not yet reaching his identified potential.

Teachers may find the works by Isaacs (*8, 9, 10, 11, 12, 14*) helpful. Articles in the **Gifted Child Quarterly** frequently focus on ways to encourage the gifted.

The writer has published a series which is useful to the teacher who has an occasional gifted child in class, or who wishes to assign readings to the whole class. The five articles in the series have several purposes. The intent is to describe some of the attributes of giftedness found in many of these individuals and then to provide reinforcement through an annotated bibliography which emphasizes and exemplifies each of the traits. Another purpose of the series is to promote the older child's analysis of the writing styles and modes of achievement of objectives employed by each author. In a sense, the series might also be regarded as "minipreventive bibliotherapy." Children who might feel too different from others in the peer group could see themselves as not altogether unusual as they encounter people with diverse talents. Preventive bibliotherapy has been noted as helpful for these purposes: 1) providing vicarious experiences, 2) extending experiences, 3) building good mental health, 4) preventing and combatting juvenile delinquency, 5) promoting developmental values, 6) forming character, 7) helping youth adjust to social and emotional situations, 8) furthering good human relations, and 9) providing a vehicle for personality growth. Reading lists need to be provided to give students materials which discuss the traits of gifted people and reinforce their development.

Enrichment Activities

For the classroom teacher and the reading teacher, the author suggests careful selection of specific activities to meet individual gifted children's needs. The following tasks, many suggested to the author by creative graduate students during past years, appear to be valuable:

1. Keep a diary describing memorable experiences.
2. Write original verses, using interesting forms of poetry such as the tanka or the Japanese Haiku and utilizing pictures or observations from the classroom window as stimulation.
3. Write stories about different phases of growing up, such as "Important Happenings," "Important People in My Life," "My Library," and "The Most Exciting Event of My Life."
4. Make collections of myths, legends, mottoes, and proverbs.
5. Study the history of languages.
6. Use different materials, such as supplemental books on a topic, Landmark Books, Merrill Company Literature Series, encyclopedias, newspapers, book sections of Sunday newspapers, editorials, sets of supplemental science books, and magazines such as *Reader's Digest, National Geographic, Popular Science, Time,* and *Newsweek.*
7. Keep records for class activities: committee membership, lists of jobs to be done, materials to be used.
8. If the class is read a story with a definite geographical locale or other specialized content, become a specialist on the subject before the class reads the story.
9. Read and discuss fine pieces of literature appropriate to interests and maturity level.
10. Listen to excellent recordings of poetry and prose.
11. Chair a committee to discuss a good book which all have read.
12. Visit a lower grade and discuss a story to stimulate interest in reading.
13. Plan and build a personal library.
14. Catalog personal books.

15. Catalog the books in a classroom library.
16. Develop an up-to-date list related to a favorite hobby or interest.
17. Compile a bibliography of interesting books for the class to use for summer reading.
18. Arrange displays for book fairs, for parents, and for other classes in the school.
19. Implement a program for the school, such as costumed book parades, quiz shows, puppet shows, and/or character sketches.
20. Organize a junior "great books club," enabling several students to discuss a book that had been read by all.
21. Set up a book swap-shop for either loans or trades.
22. Check reading rate; then use materials designed to improve rate, and chart progress.
23. Keep an individual account of materials read with notations.
24. Set up evaluative criteria, evaluate children's magazines, and make a recommended list for the library.
25. Compare the illustrations in different editions of fairy tales.
26. Report on the works and style of a favorite author.
27. Construct crossword puzzles which utilize specific vocabulary.
28. Create and play language games which involve new words or words with multiple meanings, or games using the dictionary.
29. Compile a reading notebook containing excerpts which are unusually expressive.
30. View a television program; check facts presented in written materials with those given on the program.
31. Form a poetry club which enables members to discuss favorite poems, memorize well-known poems, or compose original poems.
32. Write dramatizations and stories of historical events.
33. Participate in all phases of theater production (directing, stage lighting, stagecraft, acting).
34. Read widely to select material suitable for plays, tableaus, monologues, and puppet shows; do research necessary for staging the production.
35. Make tape recordings of oral presentations to help in self-evaluation and improvement.
36. Interview an adult or pupil from an upper grade with specific questions in mind; organize the information received for later presentation to the class.
37. Create and stage a comic opera.
38. Direct and participate in creative dramatics and choral speaking.
39. Portray a character role in a monologue.
40. Tell a story through a sequence of pictures, pantomime, dance, tableaus, dramatizations, or choral speaking.
41. In presentations, use handcrafts such as puppetry, dioramas, stage settings, costumed dolls, shadow screen, or feltboard cutouts.
42. Select and prepare a story for sharing orally with another grade group or with the class.

43. Practice public speaking by giving two-minute impromptu speeches; keep a file of possible topics.
44. Discuss a children's theater presentation; tell how the plot developed and analyze character development.
45. Explain with clarity a technical subject, such as a factory operation or some astronomical phenomenon.
46. Plan and give explicit directions for playing a game, making an object, organizing activities, or carrying out science experiments.
47. Read aloud various types of poetry, observing rules of poetic expression.
48. Give commentaries for silent movies, filmstrips, or slide showings.
49. Plan and present a play for a particular age group.
50. Learn to distinguish between statements of fact and opinion; by giving supporting evidence, prove that an article is based on one or the other.
51. Make a display showing examples of various propaganda techniques.
52. Make a comparison between getting information by listening and obtaining it from reading; compare the devices used in the two media.
53. Analyze two talks on the same subject; try to determine why one was more interesting than the other.
54. Learn to take notes from reading or a lecture; learn to outline and to summarize.
55. Document research, using bibliographies, footnotes, and quotations.
56. Compile bibliographies for several topics or events, or about subjects of interest.
57. Make constructive evaluations of televised or school programs which the class has viewed.
58. Make up and tell tall tales.
59. Tape record speeches and reports and allow class members to listen individually at a later time.
60. Make oral or written reports of attendance at concerts, plays, and visits to museums.
61. Write book reviews and character sketches.
62. Write news stories, editorials, special columns, and advertisements for a school newspaper, a class newspaper, or a large wall-mounted newspaper.
63. Assemble and edit material for school or class newspapers, scrapbooks, or social studies units.
64. Write letters requesting materials for class use on units or topics being studied.
65. Take 5-10 minutes to write about anything, or to write about something (real or imaginary) that happened yesterday, or to describe something seen on the way to school.
66. Look at some objects (tree or landscape) until something is noted that was not seen before; write new impressions.
67. Express in writing feelings about music, paintings, or other art creations.

68. Write unfinished stories to be completed by another person.
69. Select a character from a favorite story and create a new story.
70. Correspond with hospitalized veterans, particularly at holiday seasons.
71. Prepare scrapbooks of information and materials to exchange with children from other parts of the country or world.
72. Design unusual invitations to class parties or programs.
73. Write letters to imaginary friends about fictitious travels.
74. Imagine another period or place; write letters describing the setting.
75. Write an imaginary letter from one story character to another, telling something which happened after the story ended.
76. Write and illustrate stories, using local events, pictures, music, personal friends, or favorite story characters.
77. Conduct committee and class meetings.
78. Introduce guest speakers.
79. Use parliamentary procedures when suitable.
80. Write plays, poetry, descriptions, biographies, and autobiographies.
81. Convert a short story into a short play.
82. Create a poem about a painting seen in a book or a gallery.
83. Try writing a variety of story types and verse forms such as the fable, myth, parable, ode, ballad, limerick, riddle, and/or couplet.
84. Make a magazine for the classroom by compiling voluntary contributions.
85. Collect folklore, such as rope-jumping rhymes, counting-out rhymes, legends, and folk songs.
86. Make a collection of favorite poems.
87. Study the origin and derivation of words, names, places, persons, and flowers.
88. Create characters for a continued story, adding episodes from time to time.
89. Write descriptions of unusual events, animals, and people; place these in a looseleaf notebook for sharing.
90. Participate in dramatic clubs, literary clubs, storytelling clubs, and book fairs.
91. Write an article persuading people to a point of view by using biased words and appropriate propaganda.
92. Write scripts for radio programs.
93. Participate in and produce radio and television programs.
94. Analyze the point of view of an author in a particular book; read about the author in order to explain it.
95. Organize a file box for new words, arranging them under headings such as "Descriptive Words," "Words with More Than One Meaning," or "Additions to the Language."

SUMMARY

Gifted children frequently develop personal, social, or educational problems as a result of their divergent, creative behavior. While their needs at each stage of development are many, teachers are in a special position to provide an environment that will free these children to learn in terms of their own interests, styles, and rates. Through a carefully planned reading program—expanded to include all of the language arts areas—the teacher may guide gifted children toward the personal, social, and academic successes for which they have the potential.

For gifted children, adaptations of the regular classroom program must be made. There are benefits to be derived from individualized programs, linguistic study, creative reading programs, flexible language arts programs, and bibliotherapy. Also, there are numerous special activities suitable for individual children.

References

1. Arnold, Lois V. "I'll Never Forget *What's His Name*," in Helen K. Smith (Ed.), *Meeting Individual Needs in Reading*. Newark, Delaware: International Reading Association, 1971, 133-144.
2. Bamman, Henry A. "Language Arts for the Academically Talented," in Helen K. Smith (Ed.), *Meeting Individual Needs in Reading*. Newark, Delaware: International Reading Association, 1971, 143-149.
3. Barbe, Walter B. *Educator's Guide to Personalized Reading Instruction*. Englewood Cliffs, New Jersey: Prentice-Hall, 1961.
4. Duker, Sam. *Individualized Reading: Readings*. Metuchen, New Jersey: Scarecrow Press, 1969.
5. Durkin, Dolores. *Children Who Read Early*. New York: Teachers College Press, Columbia University, 1966.
6. Ehrlich, Virginia A. *Teaching Literature to the Gifted*. New York: Board of Education, City of New York, 1970.
7. Furr, Oneta R. "Improving Flexibility in Reading for the Advanced Student," in Helen K. Smith (Ed.), *Meeting Individual Needs in Reading*. Newark, Delaware: International Reading Association, 1971, 124-132.
8. Isaacs, Ann F. "For Gifted Boys' and Girls' Personality Growth and Writing Skills," *Gifted Child Quarterly*, 12 (1968), 47-49.
9. Isaacs, Ann F. "Gifted Children Benefit from Learning to be Self-Accepting," *Gifted Child Quarterly*, 12 (1968), 85-88.
10. Isaacs, Ann F. "Leadership and Ability to Accept Responsibility are Among the Most Important Attributes of the Gifted," *Gifted Child Quarterly*, 12 (1968), 227-229.
11. Isaacs, Ann F. "Self-Sufficiency is a Trait which Many Use in Describing the Gifted," *Gifted Child Quarterly*, 12 (1968), 181-182.
12. Isaacs, Ann F. "Vocabulary Enrichment for Which We Can Thank the Greeks," *Gifted Child Quarterly*, 15 (1971), 311-312.
13. Isaacs, Ann F. "Should the Gifted Preschool Child be Taught to Read?" *Gifted Child Quarterly*, 5 (1963), 72-77.

14. Isaacs, Ann F. "Special for Boys and Girls and Their Adults," *Gifted Child Quarterly*, 11 (1967), 252-253.
15. Krippner, Stanley, and C. Heald. "Reading Disabilities Among the Academically Talented," *Gifted Child Quarterly*, 7 (1964), 12-20.
16. Marckwart, A. H. (Ed.). *Linguistics in School Programs*. Chicago, Illinois: National Society for the Study of Education, 1970.
17. Pilon, A. Barbara. "Pick a Peck of Picture Books," *Gifted Child Quarterly*, 16 (1972), 11-17.
18. Spalding, Robert L. "Personalized Education in Southside Schools," *Elementary School Journal*, January 1970, 180-189.
19. Robinson, F. P. "Study Skills for Superior Students in Secondary Schools," in L. E. Hafner (Ed.), *Improving Reading in Secondary Schools*. New York: Macmillan, 1967, 175-180.
20. U. S. Office of Education, *Education of the Gifted and Talented*. Report to Congress by the U. S. Commissioner of Education and background papers submitted to the U. S. Office of Education. Washington, D. C.: U. S. Government Printing Office, 1972 (72-502 0).
21. Williamson, Ann. "Personalized Reading Progress—Multi-Aged Nongrading," in Helen K. Smith (Ed.), *Meeting Individual Needs in Reading*. Newark, Delaware: International Reading Association, 1971, 36-42.

FOSTERING CREATIVITY IN CHILDREN WHO DIFFER

Michael Labuda
Jersey City State College

and

Helen J. James
The University of West Florida

Gifted and creative children, those who are identified and labeled, appear to comprise a unique population. They have in common characteristics which permit them to approach situations without preformed ideas; to produce unusual solutions to problems; and to view the world of reality in ways that result in fresh, open-ended, or divergent consequences. On the other hand, creative children vary considerably in measured intelligence, aptitudes, and interests. As a total group, they are probably more different than they are alike, at least in ways that can be observed and measured.

During the past twelve years, gifted and creative children have been found among children who are classified as 1) minority group members or 2) learning disabled children. Such children are rarely categorized as gifted or creative and may be described in derogatory terms, such as "nonconforming" or "clever in nonacademic ways." That these children exist is a matter of record; that they exist and are not identified as gifted or creative prior to being classified in another way calls attention to the high value given to academics. In another sense, the failure to identify these children points up our narrow, limited views of what constitutes a child who "differs."

It is the purpose of this chapter to explore, albeit briefly and conservatively, the needs of children who, had they not been first classified as either culturally disadvantaged or learning disabled, could and should be members of the diverse group of gifted and creative children. It will be noted that provisions for such children demand a special kind of teacher, yet one who might well be little different from the competent, ingenious teacher who attempts to meet the needs of all children.

NEEDS OF CHILDREN CLASSIFIED AS "MINORITY GROUP MEMBERS"

The Results of History

The views of Americans toward newcomers have fluctuated over the years. Initially, immigrants who spoke many different languages were assumed to enter the mainstream of a typical America and emerge as Americans, all essentially alike and all speaking standard American English. It would appear that other nations of the world had similar expectations of permanent settlers, or the expectation that large settling groups would assimilate native subgroups, the end result being a relatively homogeneous population.

In all instances where countless immigrants joined a populace in a melting-pot situation, the transformation was far more myth than fact. In many cases, a bicultural style developed, with various subgroups coexisting and influencing each other over a long period of time. As a result, nations of the world must now come to grips with the meaning of a multicultural society.

In a pluralistic society, minorities feel somewhat threatened by the dominant groups; thus, they move into closed ethnic circles. They develop ways of behaving that are mutually acceptable, successful, and inclusive of the customs and language required within the closed group.

The child whose thoughts and language differ from the norms of an academic world into which he is thrust cannot avoid confusion, failure, and personality disintegration if he is expected to conform to the norms of his new world. For the culturally different child who possesses talents and demonstrates creative ways of coping with a variety of problems in his own subculture, there seems to be an almost instantaneous sensitivity and insight concerning school conditions that force him to conceal his abilities. He may adopt silence as his mode of response, or he may become aggressive about things in general; he may resist with surprising strength any attempt to draw him out. Consequently, he will be categorized as "culturally disadvantaged" and relegated to programs that are compensatory rather than enriching. Unless something occurs to cause him to reveal his giftedness, he continues on his self-selected, obscure, and relatively safe course.

Types of Divergence

Some households within minority groups are not child-centered; that is, normally no adult takes time to play or to talk with the child. Each child is expected to grow up as quickly as possible and to make his own way. He learns the quickest way to survive with a minimum of thought and conversation. However, a highly technological and achievement-oriented society requires complex thinking and language ability. To succeed, and the norm pushes for success, each individual's intellect must include the capacity for complex conceptualization. If possible, socialization should occur early to promote that complex development. Such conditions as poverty, limited perceptual experiences, and concrete modes of thinking and speaking greatly retard concept development.

Deprivations, whether economic or experiential, breed poverty of the intellect, leading to an inability to utilize educational and vocational opportunities, even when equitable social programs are available. Bruner and his associates (2) conclude that the research concerning symbolic intellectual development (i.e., language processes of all types) supports the hypothesis that culture influences modes of thinking and that the simpler the society, the less advancement one expects of children from that society. Since minority groups have restricted verbal explicitness and concrete, condensed meanings, families depend on extra verbal signals rather than symbols.

Bernstein (1) states that elaborated codes tend to be more universalistic and restricted codes, more particularistic. The implication for low socioeconomic groups is almost automatic failure of children, even before they begin, in a school system which emphasizes middle-class standards, which tend to be more universalistic. Deutsch (3) notes that, because the culture of many minority groups is different from the culture that has molded the school and its educational theories and practices, children from minority groups come to school so poorly prepared that failure is inevitable.

The view of giftedness as a product of superior opportunity has led to a more careful examination of environmental factors. It has been demonstrated that improved economic status, hence greater opportunities, has increased the production of minority groups. In addition, such factors as family values and interaction patterns, child-rearing practices, and self-concepts have been found to affect the development of individual children. It may be said that a variance from the norm of many factors will create problems (5).

In some minority groups, the male is supposed to be the dominant person; in other groups, the female assumes the dominant role. In one-parent families, there is bound to be a problem of identification as well as problems concerning passivity and dependency. There is often lack of communication between male and female; women are often lonely and isolated, consequently hostile. Discipline is frequently harsh and physical; getting caught for a violation of rules is a crime rather than a misdemeanor. The care of children is custodial; in many cases, any custodian is acceptable.

Strong peer-group affiliations supply social and emotional release, as well as friends, for both sexes and for both the young and old. Mothers try to encourage upward mobility, whereas fathers more often discourage it. Families are not likely to provide suitable occupational role models for their children. Thus, if a child aspires to a higher level than his parents, he has to rely on an exceptional relative, on the school, on movies, or on television for information as to what it is like to go to college or to work in a chosen profession. Several writers believe that peer-group influences take over very early in a child's life. It can be inferred that children learn early to tune out the examples and arguments of well-intentioned adults.

There are other kinds of divergent behavior found among minority groups: great skill with oral language but little skill with written language, almost indestructible loyalty within family groups, and philosophical leanings that verge on bigotry or fanaticism. Certainly, children from groups exhibiting those behaviors will not fit the norms of most schools.

The types of divergence which concern us most, regardless of other aspects of minority group children's behaviors, are those which reveal needs-meeting and/or problem-solving abilities indicative of unusual insight and unique thought. At times, the means by which a child plays a silent role, "acts out" his feelings of hostility, or resists authority are so creative that he is viewed by his teacher, as well as his peers, as a "very brilliant kid." In some instances, the handcraft products or the storytelling skills of a child give evidence of giftedness. Frequently, the nature of the child's questions suggests that his vision of possibilities exceeds the expectancies for his age group.

Those who seek the unique child among minority groups in kindergarten and primary grade classrooms usually find him. His uniqueness is revealed to a great extent in the nature of the products he creates, not necessarily in the degree of perfection he exhibits. Occasionally, however, a child reveals his creativity by his lengthy attention to a task, refusing to stop a project even for lunch after having worked all morning without having had breakfast or a snack. A few children reveal enormous cravings for certain kinds of activities that require active and thoughtful participation and very specific results, demonstrating a tenacity and a thirst for understanding far beyond normal.

One must not forget that these minority children may have combinations of divergence that seem almost incompatible in terms of traditional educational programs. To be gifted and to seek actively for knowledge, yet to lack expressive vocabulary and be ignorant of basic social behaviors, will cause conflict in the child at the same time that his behavior causes consternation to his teacher. Hence, there is need for identifying *all* aspects of divergence within an individual child.

The Role of the School

To fulfill its obligation to culturally different children, the school must become sensitive to the unique needs of these children. This sensitivity means recognizing, accepting, and interpreting cues from the learner; seeking further information to clarify cues; and adapting instruction to the cues. This process will strengthen the dignity of the individual at the same time that it enables the school to observe and document specific behaviors. When a child is treated as an important and respectable individual—one with feelings, attitudes, and experiences that are worthy of some attention—his positive strengths will be recognized first, with the inventory of his deficits coming later.

Sensitivity leads to long-range diagnosis and planning. To know the child and to fit the program to his needs are imperative. Skills of observation are essential; checklists, inventories of various types, anecdotal records, skills assessments, and tentative statements of diagnosis must be employed. Then, the implementation of a suitable program requires extensive knowledge of various approaches and techniques as well as an attitude of willingness to adapt constantly to assure success. Most of all, the teacher must understand how to utilize a child's strengths in order to overcome his weaknesses.

Fantini and Weinstein (*6*) challenge educators to meet the common needs of all children without sacrificing individuality or cultural diversity. They suggest three major areas.

1. *Teaching the basic skills and concepts needed to understand the world.* These "learning how to learn" skills include convergent and divergent thinking, problem solving, and other similar process skills.
2. *Focusing on each child's individual talents, interests, and innate abilities.* The content would come from the child rather than from the school, although the school would provide experiences to enlarge the child's interests.
3. *Utilizing group interaction, participation, and inquiry activities devoted to affective learning.* Through this suggested approach, children will acquire learning for career orientation, parenthood, citizenship, and self-development—all necessary for each individual in every culture and subculture and to the total society of a diverse population.

As a result of increased sensitivity, careful diagnosis, adaptation of instruction, and focus on the three areas just described, the school will meet the needs of all children to a greater extent. In addition, it should be possible to identify and to plan individualized instruction for children who give evidence of giftedness.

Ideally, the school will exemplify by its own diversity of approaches the fact that it respects divergence and uniqueness. On the other hand, it may be more important during initial stages of change to give attention to one aspect only: learning to observe children with thoroughness and zeal. Out of the observations should emerge data that will determine plans for instruction—plans for individual classrooms and plans for the entire school, with plans for gifted and creative children in both.

NEEDS OF LEARNING DISABLED CHILDREN
Intelligence Versus Learning Abilities

There is considerable agreement today that certain children whose measured intelligence is normal or superior fail to learn academic skills because of significant deficits in perception, conceptualization, or verbal/nonverbal expressive abilities. Lerner (8) summarizes the various types of problems and individual theories that eventually led to the following definition of learning disabilities formulated by the National Advisory Committee on Handicapped Children in 1968 (9):

> Children with special learning disabilities exhibit a disorder in one or more of the basic psychological processes involved in understanding or using spoken or written languages. These may be manifested in disorders of listening, thinking, talking, reading, writing, spelling or arithmetic. They include conditions which have been referred to as perceptual handicaps, brain injury, minimal brain dysfunction, dyslexia, developmental aphasia, etc. They do not include learning problems which are due primarily to visual, hearing, or motor handicaps, to mental retardation, emotional disturbance, or to environmental disadvantage.

The definition excludes children who fail to learn because of low intelligence, emotional deprivation, environmental deprivation, or physiological sensory handicaps. It includes, in essence, children of normal and superior intelligence who do not perform in school according to their potential despite what can be assumed to be an adequate instructional program. The definition implies careful diagnosis before labeling a child. The estimate of incidence of children with specific learning disabilities is 1-3 percent of the school population (9).

Some interesting facts appear in the literature concerning certain learning disabled children: During preschool years, these children exhibited extraordinary curiosity about their world; they demonstrated creativity and certain specific talents. Some were called "highly verbal"; others were described as "scientifically inclined" or "talented in mathematical activities." Neither parents of such children nor their kindergarten teachers envisioned difficulties in academic learning. In past years, many teachers have delayed referring such children for diagnosis because they had evidence of good intellectual functioning in many respects, even if the children were failing to master basic skills of abstract symbolization. Notations on school records would suggest that "in a year or two" these children would settle down to academics and make good progress. That they did not make gains in achievement caused anxieties among children, parents, and teachers. As a result, many children acquired either poor attitudes toward school or severe emotional disturbance.

While not all learning disabled children demonstrate creativity or unusual talent, there are many who do. In fact, some make up for inadequacies in learning abilities by compensating in such an unusual fashion that they mask their problems for years. For example, a child who cannot learn to spell will produce illegible handwriting, at the same time discussing his ideas with clarity and excellent vocabulary; he is permitted to dictate or to tape his thoughts, receiving approval and commendation. Or a child with expressive language problems may draw intricate pictures with suitable labels, demonstrating superior talent of one type and receiving recognition for his giftedness in that area. Another child may have almost no reading ability; yet, by discussing ideas with others and listening to other children read, he will demonstrate knowledge and process ideas rapidly, even knowing precisely where a certain fact may be located on a given page.

Other learning disabled children reveal insights in particular areas, on particular topics, and/or in problem solving. When their strengths are utilized in classroom projects, they produce results that are viewed as outstanding by their peers, their parents, and their teachers. The value of their productions, especially to themselves, is confirmation of their abilities to learn; this confirmation is essential to the child who lacks a specific ability and may well be the greatest motivating factor in remediating his deficiency.

Intelligence, as measured by individual tests such as the Wechsler Intelligence Scale for Children and the Stanford-Binet Intelligence Scale, appears to be a critical indicator of potential for creativity in children with specific learning disabilities. Careful observation and extensive diagnosis will help the teacher discriminate between children and identify those with giftedness or creative ability.

The Educational Task

After a comprehensive evaluation has been made of a child's

assets and deficits, it is possible to establish educational objectives for his maximum development. These objectives should assist him with learning so that he attains his potential. To attain the objectives, he may require the services of psychologists, neurologists, ophthalmologists, and pediatricians, as well as his classroom teacher, a learning disabilities teacher, and other members of the educational staff (7).

For the learning disabled child who is gifted or creative, a major goal is correlation of efforts so that in every possible way he may pursue his interests without interruption while he also receives appropriate remediation for his disability. In most instances, the classroom activities at his age or grade level will enable him to produce creatively, provided the adults directing his selection of projects understand how to use his strengths and overcome his weaknesses. The learning disabilities teacher can furnish diagnostic information and assist the classroom teacher in planning suitable activities.

As pointed out in preceding sections of this volume, it is essential that inspired children work on problems that challenge them, avoid boredom from inoccuous lessons, and maintain their interest in learning. Obviously, when a child does not learn certain skills easily and must practice extensively with a skilled clinician to master those skills, he verges on feelings of boredom, disinterest, inferiority, and failure. For him, successes with individual and group projects related to his interests and talents will balance his frustrations with remedial lessons and rekindle his determination to learn needed skills.

It should be clear that no individual teacher can have the time to work alone with a learning disabled child on his projects. Pairs of children, small groups, and resource persons can accomplish much under the guidance of the teacher. Librarians, art and music teachers, and physical education instructors can assist in many ways. These coordinated efforts will require sharing of diagnostic summaries and recommendations for instruction supplied by learning disabilities teachers and other specialists.

Lerner (8) suggests that a pupil be ". . . involved in both analysis of his problem and evaluation of his performance. . . . [and] take an active role in designing lessons and choosing materials." This collaboration of pupil and teacher on a continuing basis builds the child's self-concept, provides evidence of his progress, and interests the child in learning. When the child also feels that his interests are acknowledged as worthy, he can view himself as what he is: a complex, unique individual with certain strengths and certain weaknesses, one who has successes and problems, one who is valued for his talents and who is helped to overcome his deficiencies.

CREATIVE TEACHING AND LEARNING FOR CHILDREN WHO DIFFER

Since minority group children and learning disabled children require adaptation of instruction in terms of their interests and needs, many educational procedures of individualization are suitable. Various aspects of creative teaching are suggested throughout this volume. The recommendations in this section apply to all gifted and creative learners but especially to children who differ in the special ways discussed in this chapter.

Personalizing Instruction

The creative teacher seeks to make learning relevant by inviting children's active participation in planning and implementing activities in which they are interested. The teacher uses his knowledge of pupils' interests and needs to introduce the processes in the general curriculum; pupils select the content to be used in teaching the required skills.

This approach to instruction, intended to assure each child that his personal interests will be met, requires the teacher to be grounded in the structure of knowledge rather than in a mass of facts. The teacher's command of this structure enables him to adapt it for his pupils and to relate it to their own reality. The results will be divergent, open-ended, and meaningful to each individual child in terms of his personal involvement.

The respect for children's uniqueness and the provision of interesting experiences combine to free children so that they express themselves in various ways. They appreciate not only their own products but also the products of others; they see value in diverseness, and they learn from it. Given encouragement, they develop new means of communication, whether by spoken language, pantomime, or artistic endeavor. Eventually, they gain a clearer awareness of themselves and the world in which they live.

The child who is culturally different begins to move into reading and writing in a natural way, for he develops a need to obtain information and a willingness to learn the skills. As he works with other children who have academic skills, he gains a conviction that he can learn the skills as well as others. If instruction is adapted to suit his learning style and rate, he gradually becomes a reader, a writer, and a speller. Then, his creativity can be released in additional ways.

While the learning disabled child may not need the motivation to want to learn academic skills, he does need to involve himself in academic tasks, if only vicariously, partly because some elements of skills learning will be absorbed but mostly because he is a member of the in-group achieving a goal. Often, his strength will enable him to suggest the creative touch to a project or to carry out a particular segment for which he possesses the needed abilities. His interests find fulfillment, and he maintains the momentum needed to sustain him during the period of remediation of his deficiency.

Attempting to verbalize without specific examples limits the meaning of individualizing or personalizing. The next part of this section supplies samples of creative behavior.

Imaginative Results

Real satisfaction in learning comes from the joy of creation and the solving of a problem or transforming an idea into reality. It also comes from activities which are interesting and worthy of a child's attention and concern and within his range of maturity.

An intermediate grade disadvantaged group from an urban Jersey City setting were encouraged to draw upon their repertoire of experiences as they became concerned with the problem of pollution besetting society. They expressed their feelings and arranged their ideas in a pattern that was different from any previous pattern in their thinking; they wrote the following:

Pollution

People, people, what do you see?
I see pollution enveloping me.
Pollution, pollution, what do you see?
I see people making money off of me.
Money, money, what do you see?
I see industry loving me.
Industry, industry, what do you see?
I see fish dying because of me.
Fish, fish, what do you see?
I see animals joining me.

A creative fourth grade child from another urban disadvantaged setting was encouraged to experiment with ideas. She freely associated humor in her imaginings and related seemingly impossible situations.

The Gooma Looma Binta Boo

This strange creature is found in lakes and streams. He is a playful animal, but is known for his raging temper when tickled.

One reason the Gooma Looma Binta Boo is strange is because he has two heads, one arm, and six pink and yellow legs. He eats rocks, pebbles, and any kind of hard tasty food that he can munch on. I recommend him for a pet because he is friendly and loves children. I know; he just had my kid brother for lunch!

An eighth grade disadvantaged girl from an urban Philadelphia setting always resisted but never with any determined show of will or anger. She was labeled by her teachers as a nonperformer. In a playful, yet purposeful, behavior, she sought a solution to saving the few trees found in cities by writing this:

A Day in the Life of a Tree

"It's great to get those nasty leaves off of me. They were bothering me all summer. Now I can relax.... Oh, no! As we say in IOT (International Organization of Trees)." SLIT. "It's a slitter, dreadful enemy of me, a tree. Oh, that horrible carving knife. No initials, please!" SLIT. "Oh, pain, pain, pain!" SLIT! SLIT! SLIT! "Oh, stop, please stop! There's an R penetrating my twentieth ring, an M on my twenty-second, and an M slaughtering my eighteenth. RMN. Who could that be?? IOT will get him!"

As illustrated by these examples, children labeled as failures can meet with considerable success in their attempts to reveal their insights into situations. Hearing good literature, discussing ideas in an open environment, and having freedom to manipulate language to suit their fancies can elicit unique productions.

The ways in which learning disabled children communicate when they cannot spell and write frequently surprise teachers. A third grade girl was absolutely undaunted by the class assignment to write a personal letter. She rapidly drew a series of rough sketches to communicate a series of thoughts, then added "Dear" followed by a smiling face to the beginning and "Love" and her initials at the end. Asked to read her letter, she clearly stated a sentence for each sketch. Her letter was admired by her classmates, and she glowed with satisfaction.

Letter writing seems to have a special appeal to young children and may be a means of accomplishing reading goals in unexpected ways. One second grade boy who was unable to sit still for reading activities proceeded to learn many words as he spent much of each day writing letters to the teacher, his classmates, and visitors to his classroom. Apparently, the motor activity of writing met a need to be moving. Having to find out how to spell the words he needed gave him interaction with other children, and writing the words impressed them on his memory so that he gained a good reading and spelling vocabulary. He vegan to identify words in reading materials; and even if he had to walk around while doing his reading, he began to spend time reading to himself and to anyone who would listen.

An unusually creative six-year-old inner city boy surprised school personnel by drawing complicated pictures and dictating stories of over one hundred words within a few weeks after he entered school. He was happy to have his picture and story mounted; he would point out his story, but he would never sit to have it read to him nor try to identify any word in it. He taped stories and constructed his own setting and characters to dramatize the tale. He learned number facts, but he did not write them. After five months, his teacher bargained with him to get five minutes' effort in readiness activities leading to writing for each thirty minutes he had for his special projects. It became apparent that he was an expert judge of his disability, for his early writing revealed reversals, rotations, omissions, and substitutions. However, he made slow and genuine progress in recognizing letters and forming them. Gradually, he began to label his own pictures. He did not become a member of a reading group until the sixth month of second grade, when he suddenly seemed to have confidence in his ability to cope with what he called "a bunch of words." The individualized program had prevented failure and encouraged his efforts.

It may be that learning problems will fail to develop if teachers view each child as unique in his rate, style, and pattern of learning and allow him to choose his own values and interests. Drews (4) states:

> By honoring these directions of growth and allowing them to flourish naturally, we found that students could master what had been difficult topics and materials and do this easily. As we have seen, a nonreader began to read without the pressure of applied methods and scheduled class periods. Students who habitually failed English found they could speak fluently and well when they could talk about something of interest rather than on an assigned topic. Just as the school came to a close, a boy who had been an indifferent mathematics student did four months' work in three days and ended up six weeks ahead of his classmates.

SUMMARY

Minority group children and learning disabled children are sometimes gifted or creative, although they are not first recognized as talented because their academic failures override whatever creativity they may demonstrate. Special attention that involves thorough diagnosis and individualized instruction may permit such children to live up to their creative potential as well as master needed basic skills.

Children from minority groups have divergent language, conceptualization abilities, and/or life styles that cause failure when they enter the traditional school setting. Yet some of these children reveal problem-solving abilities or needs-meeting talents indicative of unusual insight and unique thought. The school must provide the means for good observation, diagnosis, and adaptation of instruction to prevent failure and to encourage these children in following their interests.

Learning disabled children have normal or superior intelligence accompanied by a specific deficit in perception, conceptualization, or receptive or expressive language abilities. Some of these children are extremely creative in compensating for a deficiency; others are particularly talented in one area of learning, such as mathematics or science. The educational task is twofold: The child's strengths must be utilized in challenging, rewarding ways; his weaknesses must be overcome through expert remediation.

Personalized instruction will promote the learning of processes required in the general curriculum, at the same time assuring children that their personal interests are valuable and will be met. Both minority group children and learning disabled children will create unique products as teachers adapt their instruction to meet specific needs of children. The results of their creative endeavors will be diverse, ranging from imaginative writing to handcraft and art.

References

1. Bernstein, Basil. "Social Class and Linguistic Development: A Theory of Social Learning," in A. H. Halsey, J. Floud, and C. A. Anderson (Eds.), *Education, Economy, and Society*. New York: Free Press of Glencoe, 1961.
2. Bruner, Jerome S. et al. *Studies in Cognitive Growth*. New York: John Wiley and Sons, 1966.
3. Deutsch, Martin. "The Disadvantaged Child and the Learning Process," in A. H. Passow (Ed.), *Education in Depressed Areas*. New York: Teachers College Press, Columbia University, 1963.
4. Drews, Elizabeth Monroe. *Learning Together: How to Foster Creativity, Self-Fulfillment, and Social Awareness in Today's Students and Teachers*. Englewood Cliffs, New Jersey: Prentice-Hall, 1972.
5. *Education of the Gifted and Talented*. Report to Congress by the U. S. Commissioner of Education and background papers submitted to the U. S. Office of Education. Washington, D.C.: U. S. Government Printing Office, 1972. (72-502 0)
6. Fantini, Mario, and Gerald Weinstein. *The Disadvantaged*. New York: Holt, Rinehart and Winston, 1968.
7. Johnson, Doris J., and Helmer R. Myklebust. *Learning Disabilities: Educational Principles and Practices*. New York: Grune and Stratton, 1967.
8. Lerner, Janet. *Children with Learning Disabilities: Theories, Diagnosis, and Teaching Strategies.* Boston: Houghton Mifflin, 1971, 76.
9. National Advisory Committee on Handicapped Children. *Special Education for Handicapped Children*. First Annual Report. Washington, D.C.: U. S. Department of Health, Education, and Welfare, 1968.

PART FIVE

A LOOK AHEAD

Implementing change requires a serious examination of our philosophy and a clarification of problems and recommendations for meeting the individual needs of the gifted and creative as we foster reading growth. This brief glimpse of encouraging trends coupled with recommendations for an open, flexible, creative atmosphere provides a ray of light into the future. The present needs of the gifted and the creative have reached the crisis stage. Carefully planned provisions are needed. The individual, the school, and all concerned will be stimulated to undertake widespread efforts on behalf of the gifted and creative student. By extending and enriching significant contributions in the area of creative reading we will assure the leadership we want and need as we move into the 2000s.

M.L.

FORGING AHEAD IN READING FOR GIFTED AND CREATIVE LEARNERS

Michael Labuda
Jersey City State College

The painstaking study by the U. S. Office of Education (cited in Chapter 1), has confirmed the impression of inadequate provisions for gifted and creative learners and the widespread misunderstanding about their needs. However, out of this dismal picture comes a light of hope. National, state, and local educators, in cooperation with concerned parents, have banded together in long-range comprehensive planning to rectify some of the major deficiencies.

The emphasis on humanism is an encouraging trend. There is an openness in education that encourages tomorrow's minds (rather than attempting to reproduce yesterday's minds) as children are freed to focus on the unsolved parts of the curriculum rather than on the solved parts. Learning experiences appear to be moving beyond memorization and simple cognition toward the advanced skill of interpreting in one's own words what an answer might be. The learner can live more fully in classroom worlds that are filled with children's purposes. The thinking of each child, accepted as represented in his own language, serves as a basic ingredient for the production of reading materials which assure personal meaning. With this freedom, the learner is able to develop fully his own dimensions of learning in a creative way and to have a better opportunity to meet his needs and wants without fear of rejection.

Parents are actively involved in establishing programs, and in many states education departments have appointed key personnel to be responsible for programs for the gifted. Striving to be truly accountable, more teachers are seeking to evaluate all children on the basis of their potential rather than on their status in a group. All who are aware of the educational process are coming to infer that much of the available material can be adapted to meet the reading needs of gifted and creative learners.

Teachers want to strike the initial spark of interest; they want to provide creative and imaginative experiences for their students. Consequently, demands are increasing for creative workshops and inservice courses and teachers are learning a variety of techniques to stimulate children's thinking. This eagerness of teachers to stimulate gifted and creative pupils will result in originality and renewed interest in learning.

Although programs are inadequate to accommodate all the gifted and creative, it is encouraging that there is generally a broader concept of giftedness which includes a capacity for high level creative responses. Schools must continue, extend, and more fully develop programs where they already exist; other schools must identify and encourage creative learners by initiating substantial programs for the gifted.

We cannot become complacent after observing the encouraging signs of progress. We are far from the target of providing maximum development of every child in accordance with his unique nature and needs.

The gifted and creative child needs individually suited and interesting reading experiences from the beginning of his entrance into school. Reading should be considered as experiencing, thinking, and learning throughout the entire day, using varied sources that are challenging and appealing. This must, of course, include exposure to learning situations that go beyond the textbook. Experience with different media will create excitement in the development of skills and positive attitudes that are too often absent in the learning process. All these experiences in reading must be correlated with activities in creative writing and self-expression in multiple media, since the child learns to read and refines skills in many ways. In this way the child can develop his interests and concerns by choosing suitable reading materials, he can become increasingly able to establish his own purpose for reading, and eventually can refine his reading skills.

Manpower needs of a nation are not the same today as they will be in the future. Reading, however, is a prerequisite for successful living in our society. As educators, we build upon past successes as we innovate change to accommodate our particular needs. Good programs for the gifted and creative have been reported in many books and journals and these programs stand as examples of the best that education can presently offer. Dedicated teachers are recognizing individual differences and are practicing personalized instruction which satisfies varied interests and needs of the gifted and creative child. Techniques such as the open classroom, nongradedness, team teaching, multimedia, and new types of textbooks extend and enrich opportunities for the gifted and creative child and also provide more adequate and stimulating experiences for the disadvantaged. Daily attention and exposure to a variety of materials will provide reading improvement through useful interaction with specific skills. A unit approach to teaching and learning can be very effective and efficient. Teachers can select those activities which are immediately useful or pertinent to the subject matter currently being taught in the classroom to supplement, enrich, and expand their present instructional program. In our concern with the development of higher levels of literacy, we must keep in mind that concepts are of greater significance than a particular approach or set of materials.

In every class, opportunities should be available and guidance offered, so that gifted children will continue to develop reading abilities and apply them widely. Predictive abilities should receive equal emphasis with word recognition abilities as children interact with the ideas and language they meet through their readings. The understanding of linguistic bases of language, whether phonological, morphological, or syntactical, should be extended so that gifted children may understand how language works for them.

The involvement of the parent is crucial in regard to the child's learning. What goes on in the school is directly significant and directly related to the home and the kind of reinforcement and encouragement the gifted and creative child receives. Both the educational process and the educational outcome depend on what happens to the whole child; therefore, we must encouarge parent involvement. Since, in some instances, the home is not equipped to give individualized attention, the services of paraprofessionals have provided significant help. With appropriate use of paraprofessionals, highly qualified instruction can be accomplished in the schools. The important fact is that the child is getting the attention he needs as an individual, even if it is for only a few minutes a day.

We need to upgrade teacher education and inservice education. As we take giant steps forward in our efforts to teach reading from the beginning stages to the stage of refinement, we are developing reading skills and interests that will satisfy these youngsters for the rest of their lives. Therefore, it is extremely important that we have the best quality instruction and materials if we are to prepare the gifted and creative youngsters to lead our society in the 2000s.

Industry, business, government, churches, and other institutions have much to offer the gifted and creative. Professionally qualified persons such as artists, musicians, and others with special training and competencies can offer much to the total development of the gifted and creative. In addition, we might also reevaluate the kinds of programs that are being offered outside the present school setup. In particular, those gifted who have difficulties in reading need other ways of acquiring information in meeting their needs for success in reading.

The present needs of the gifted and the creative pupil are acute, and there is a need for carefully planned programs. In the year 2000 we will be dependent on the leadership abilities of our gifted and creative population; their education today and in the future must assure that they attain their full potential.

SUMMARY

The educational failure of the gifted and creative is not merely a limited problem involving only the school and the individual. If these children are to receive rewarding and beneficial experiences which contribute toward their growth, all parties involved—children, parents, administrators, teachers, and schools—must unite to provide the best quality education for all children from all socioeconomic backgrounds. An open, flexible philosophy balanced with quality teaching, quality programs, and the best materials available will provide the depth and breadth these neglected children so direly need as they become the sophisticated and well-trained leaders of the future.

The International Reading Association attempts, through its publications, to provide a forum for a wide spectrum of opinion on reading. This policy permits divergent viewpoints without assuming the endorsement of the Association.